THE ROAD TO TEXAS

The Road to Texas

Victor Prosper Considerant

Translated from the French by
Paola Tettamanzi Buckley

DEEP VELLUM PUBLISHING
DALLAS, TEXAS

Deep Vellum Publishing
3000 Commerce St., Dallas, Texas 75226
deepvellum.org · @deepvellum

Deep Vellum is a 501c3 nonprofit literary arts organization
founded in 2013 with the mission to bring
the world into conversation through literature.

Support for this publication has been provided in part by the National
Endowment for the Arts, the Texas Commission on the Arts, the City of Dallas
Office of Arts and Culture, the Communities Foundation of Texas, and the Addy
Foundation.

ISBNs: 978-1-64605-265-3 (paperback) | 978-1-64605-286-8 (ebook)

LIBRARY OF CONGRESS CATALOG NUMBER: 2024021851

Front Cover Design by Lexi Earle
Interior Layout and Typesetting by KGT

"Freedom is the lifeblood, the soul, the dignity, and the reason for which the American people exist. The American people recognize that they presently represent Freedom to the entire world and that they have become the custodians of this Freedom for humanity's foreseeable future."

CONTENTS

PART ONE
From December 1852 to May 1853

PART TWO
In Texas

PART THREE
Preparations

TRANSLATOR'S NOTE/INTRODUCTION

In 1855, Victor Considerant, a French socialist utopian, led a group of roughly two hundred French, Belgian, and Swiss immigrants to Texas following his visit to Texas the previous year. He became captivated by its splendor and the sense of freedom and optimism he experienced within its borders. In his book *The Road to Texas!*, Considerant outlined his plan to establish a socialist utopian community in an area along the Trinity River, about three miles west of what is now downtown Dallas. The settlers called their settlement La Réunion. Disillusioned with the social inequalities and political chaos that plagued Europe, Considerant and his followers pursued their version of the American Dream, which for this group of socialist utopians, signified the creation of an egalitarian, collective society.

In the wake of the French Revolution and Napoléon's Empire, France experienced persistent social, political, and ideological turmoil. In 1830, Charles X, the French Bourbon monarch, was overthrown. In 1848, following the February Revolution, France declared its Second Republic, a Constituent Assembly was formed, and Louis-Napoléon Bonaparte was elected president. In 1851, he proclaimed himself Napoléon III, Emperor of France, and established the Second French Empire that lasted until 1870.

During this same period, European intellectuals began to expound the principles of socialism and communism. Indeed, Charles Fourier (1772–1837), a French philosopher and utopian socialist, founded a school of thought in which he "advocated for communities organized into 'phalanxes' freed from private ownership in order to provide economic comfort, social justice, and individual fulfillment."[1] Several failed "phalanxes" were established in Europe and in the United States; the community of Brook Farm in Massachusetts represented another failed experiment in utopian socialism.

Victor Considerant (1808–1893), the author of *To Texas!* and the founder of La Réunion, became a disciple of Charles Fourier. Upon Fourier's death, he became the leader of Fourier's utopian socialist movement. After the February Revolution of 1848, Considerant campaigned for a seat in the newly formed Constituent Assembly; however, "Fourierism never enjoyed a large following in the working classes. Thus, Considerant, while popular with middle class intellectuals, was not a big vote-getter."[2] In 1849, Considerant was involved in the planning of an insurrection against the conservative French government. The brief uprising failed and Considerant fled Paris and moved to Brussels.

It was against this backdrop of growing industrialization

and political and social upheaval that the French utopian socialists, led by Victor Considerant, sought to establish an egalitarian community where they could live according to their common principals. In 1854, Victor Considerant visited Albert Brisbane, his American friend and fellow utopian, and they traveled to Texas, where, following the end of the Mexican-American War in 1848, Europeans, mainly Czech and German immigrants, began to settle. While they traveled along the banks of the Trinity River, in an area where the nascent city of Dallas emerged, Considerant and Brisbane found their promised land.

Considerant returned to Belgium where he published the book *To Texas!* (or *Au Texas!*, in the original French), in which he describes how his voyage led to his infatuation with Texas, and how the fertile lands of its North Central region embodied the ideal location for his utopian socialist settlement. Considerant organized the American-European Settlement Company, an investment fund that would finance the establishment of his group's new society. The fund quickly amassed five hundred thousand francs (roughly two hundred thousand current US dollars) from Belgian, Swiss and French investors, all of whom were Fourier's, and consequently Considerant's, disciples.

Considerant's description of Texas waxed so eloquently that settlers rushed to arrive, and about two hundred French, Belgian, and Swiss utopian socialists landed in Galveston in early 1855. They journeyed to Dallas by carriage and on foot, and the trip took almost six weeks.

Within the next year, around five hundred settlers arrived at La Réunion, many of whom did not fit the image of the resilient, independent pioneer who settled the American West. Many of the newcomers aspired to recreate the comforts and refinements they had left behind in Europe. One of La Réunion's settlers built a brewery and produced the first beer brewed in Dallas County. Mr. Bureau, the secretary of La Réunion, brought the first-ever piano to Dallas County for use by his family, who "were all fine musicians and added no little to the pleasure of the colonists."[3]

Unfortunately, of the five hundred colonists, there were barely a dozen farmers, prompting one settler, Mr. Cantegrel, to exclaim: "Mon Dieu! I am sent here to direct an agricultural settlement and have no agriculturists to direct."[4] Indeed, recruits were selected without much regard to their background and their ability to contribute to the growth of La Réunion. Fourierism was most popular among intellectuals, not the working class, therefore, Considerant's expedition attracted more artisans and intellectuals as opposed to farmers and tradesmen.

The lack of farming knowledge along with a severe drought led to the exhaustion of their investment funds, all of which contributed to the dissolution of La Réunion. The final disbandment came in 1858, about three years after the first settlers arrived. Some settlers remained in Dallas, some moved to other parts of Texas, others went to New Orleans, and many returned to Europe. Considerant first went to Austin and eventually returned to Paris, where he lived in the Latin Quarter, joined the International Workingmen's Association and took part in the Franco-Prussian War in 1870 and in the Paris Commune of 1871.

The dissolution of La Réunion cannot entirely be attributed to concrete occurrences such as bad weather, lack of money and inexperienced farmers. When the settlers arrived in Texas to found their socialist utopian society, they embodied the French ideals of Liberté, Égalité, Fraternité: Liberty, Equality, and Brotherhood. The idea of brotherhood in particular aligned with the socialist utopian principal of the collective community. However, as the settlers began to experience challenges and setbacks, they did not maintain the principal of brotherhood as their dream of a collective society began to erode. Indeed, "individualism was beginning to assert itself. The desire to have something as an individual, something that could be used or killed or sold without calling a town meeting to discuss the matter, was making headway against the formula of Fourier."[5]

The increased pervasiveness of individual aspirations instead of collective ambitions can be seen as a factor that contributed to La Réunion's demise. One could also infer that the settlers of La Réunion who remained in Texas adopted the principles of "Life, Liberty and the pursuit of Happiness," as the latter belief firmly exemplifies an individualistic undertaking. Considerant's blueprint was disallowed and the pursuit of a socialist utopian society in Texas was instead replaced by the pursuit of individual happiness as characterized by the American Dream.

I would like to add a final note regarding my reference to La Réunion as *a settlement* as opposed to *a colony*. In *To Texas!* Considerant uses the terms "colonie" and "colonization" to refer to the utopian society he seeks to establish in Texas. In my translation, I made the decision to use the terms *settlement* and *settlers*, lest readers be distracted by the historical implications and adverse connotations of the words "colony" and "colonization." Considerant and the French settlers of La Réunion did not come to Dallas to impose their beliefs and their model of communal society on others; they came, like many before and since, to escape political turmoil, to find freedom, and to pursue opportunities.

1. https://freethought-trail.org/causes/cause:fourierist-utopianism.

2. https://www.ohio.edu/chastain/ac/consider.htm.

3. January 25, 1891, Dallas Morning News, Pt. 3, p. 1.

4. January 25, 1891, Dallas Morning News, Pt. 3, p. 1.

5. January 25, 1891, Dallas Morning News, Pt. 3, p. 1.

FOREWORD

Be advised that this is not a book, nor is this writing destined for the general public. This is a candid, private document printed for, and addressed to, friends.

The substance of this Report will no doubt appeal to a broader public; nevertheless, it must remain faithful to our group's communally conceived, unique principals, and it must remain concomitant to the moral and intellectual lucidity of these principals. We will therefore renounce its circulation among a wider audience until we can establish a homogenous core of participants who agree to dedicate themselves to our shared social goals and to the principal Idea of our community.

The reasons mentioned above will initially determine the audience to whom we address the Proposal contained in this Essay. Given the specificity of the audience, the author at times employed the vernacular belonging to our Associative School, which may not always be intelligible to the general public. This familiarity in turn inspired the author's subtitle, *Report to My Friends.*

The Road to TEXAS

Report to My Friends

BEFORE DEPARTURE

I

When I was about to leave for the United States, toward the end of 1852, I was in the midst of writing you a dispatch in which I looked back on the sequential phases of our group's expansion and reflected on our present state of affairs. I pondered the direction that the Phalansterian School's endeavors should potentially consider, while I remained mindful of the various obstacles that currently encumber the group. Nonetheless, I identified meaningful elements, stemming from the nature of current historical developments and apparent to all of your trained minds, that can propel our organization from its past to its future.

These elements consist of, on the one hand, industry and science, and on the other hand, the progressive ideas that ensued from our contemporary social dilemmas. Any other contemporaneous element belongs to the past and has no relevance to us now.

Even though so many modern creations that result from science and industry evolve in an autonomous and contained environment, we observe how they can gradually be adapted to the Harmonic Process of Series. These elements in turn become true instruments of a prodigious, complex community. In other words, these modern creations unwittingly make their way into our Associative Social Order.

As for actual socialist ideas, despite the excitement they incited in previous times, and notwithstanding the gargantuan creative efforts put forth by their supporters to promote them, they noticeably express only shreds or distortions of Fourier's vast, homogenous, and congruous thoughts. This becomes evident once one reviews these ideas, beginning with communist doctrines, then the various variations of guarantism (a system of credits, reciprocity, trade reforms, workers coalitions, communal consumption, innovations in education, etc . . .), and finally the individual reactions of Messieurs Proudhon and Émile de Girardin.

All this enthusiastic, irrepressible, and flawed work centers around two axes:

a) The need for a perfect combination of social forces and convictions.

b) The need for unblemished and absolute liberty for all humans.

This consequently implies a third pivot:

c) A universally agreed upon system of apportionment.[1]

---

1. Today, regardless of our efforts to the contrary, it has become clear that the chief obstacles encountered by socialism derive from its obstinance to prioritize the third pivot (apportionment) over the other two axes that scientifically precede it, engender it and bring it forth.

We are all cognizant of the socialists' past disagreements over these three absolutes. Alternatively, Fourier's supported conviction that the fundamental force propelling a new Social Order is contained in the systemic and harmonious association of natural and human elements; this system clearly delineates the path forward for human civilization, since our great Social Theory presents a defined structure, the Phalanx Community, for its eventual realization.

I pondered how, given our current circumstances, we could hasten our objectives. Even though I habitually opposed any sort of feeble initiative, discussions about our present conditions have forced me to recognize that it would be preferable for our School to undertake any type of project at this moment rather than prolong our absolute inaction. This reckoning leads me to propose an experimental project based on the Harmonic Process of Series in which we would focus exclusively on the essential elements of our doctrine, and for which we would require minimal resources. The basis for this project had already been discussed and outlined in letters exchanged between myself and our friends in Paris during the summer.

Upon scrupulous deliberation, I concluded that the ensuing proposed implementation plan embodies the only visible way forward, as it contains measures that are both practicable and acceptable to our group.

II

Dear friends, I want to be clear that I have never lost my faith in our cause, and I do not for an instant doubt the ultimate triumph of Harmonious Order and the law of Series expounded by Fournier. In the past, we could justifiably expect to have the freedom and the support to undertake unconstrained experimentation to bring forth this mission. Nevertheless, due to external pressures, as a last resort, I was obliged of late to distance myself from our School. I write this so you can understand my state of mind when I left for America.

It seemed necessary to offer you this explanation so you could properly assess the plans that I present to you in these pages. I wanted to accurately describe the causes that instigated the development and concretization of my proposal, and thought it natural to communicate this to you in order to elucidate my stance.

I will therefore begin with the state of mind that surrounded my departure. All the while, I had exclusively contemplated only our European options; my voyage was still a conjecture when Brisbane paid us a visit. I did everything in my power to convince him that we should begin an experimentation in Switzerland where I believed we could unite and act expeditiously. Brisbane instead brought forth the idea of America, but I found this of little value and simply refuted his suggestion. It is true that Brisbane had already traveled across Europe five or six times and even reached Asia once; nevertheless, he was only familiar with a small portion of his own country, which we were destined to discover together a few months hence.

My goal here is neither to write a book about the United States, nor to write a travel narrative, as that would require several volumes. Rather, I will limit my observations to the information that pertains to my Proposal, which remains the objective of this Report.

PART ONE

FROM DECEMBER 1852 TO MAY 1853

I

My departure for the New World was as accidental as it was sudden. You could say that I was brought to America; indeed, I didn't deliberately choose to make the trip. When it became clear that my departure was imminent, I scarcely had time to inform my friends in Paris.

My intention was to explore the New World during a three-month period, and I had no thoughts of discovering a solution to our group's concerns. In fact, I began a proposal for an experimentation in Switzerland which I intended to complete during the transatlantic voyage; I would send it to Paris upon my arrival.

I left Antwerp on November 28, 1852, and Liverpool in December; I entered New York Bay on the evening of December 14. We had rough seas and strong head winds throughout the journey. Thanks to steamships, crossings today only take ten to eleven days, and it's easy to imagine that in a few short years these crossings will take only half as many days. The two hemispheres are moving ever closer.

In Europe, we are all, to some extent, familiar with

American society thanks to newspaper accounts and books. The reality I encountered was far more seducing than even the most faithful descriptions. A two-hour walk in New York made a deeper impact on my appreciation of its greatness than any of my previous readings about the city.

The spontaneity of human interactions; the speed of the people and the traffic they create; the brusqueness of everybody's movements; all these elements collide and create a space in which a person is constantly thrashed about. Continuous streams of organic activity emanate from every corner such as an active volcano spews forth streams of matter. The intense and constant energy produced by the mass of humanity envelops you in an instant, assaults your senses and jostles your very core. The energy of unhindered individualism and the force of personal activity that is free of obstructions resound so strongly that one becomes dazed. Immediately upon landing, the European recognizes that he has set foot onto a new world.

Nobody was waiting for me when I arrived. Our friends learned of my presence in the newspapers, which incidentally published several articles favorable to our cause and our doctrines. I attended a monthly gathering of journalists in New York, and I was welcomed amicably. Brisbane, who was in Buffalo, hastened to join me in New York.

We were entering the dead of winter and I felt the need to quiet the chaos that echoed around me and to concretize a plan. I wanted to learn a bit of English in order to prepare myself for a productive journey with Brisbane, who delighted in our upcoming adventure, therefore, before Brisbane took his leave to tend to his affairs, he accompanied me to the North American Phalanx, an associated community founded in the State of New Jersey, not far from New York. I was overjoyed at the opportunity to study the workings of this phalanx and was also thrilled by the promise of English lessons. A few words about this Association will not go to waste.

II

We repeatedly expounded on the nature and the proliferation of our school's Doctrine in America to our European friends. Let us review these circumstances. Fourier's ideology comprises two general concepts: first, the idea of *Association*, and second, the *Process of Series*. The concept of *Association* represents a cooperative and collective social and economic order, as opposed to one that is fragmented and exclusionary. The Process of Series recognizes that there exists an organic and harmonious order on which the Association is founded. In America, the spread of our Doctrine has revolved mostly around the idea of *Association*, and the ideas contained in the Process of Series have been mostly ignored.

The simplification of the Doctrine—reducing the theory to its most basic elements—facilitated the adhesion to its principles, thereby accelerating its expansion. This falls in line with Americans' inclination to forge ahead without adequate preparation. The Americans who adopted our societal principals simply stipulated that gathering together on a plot of land and pledging to live together in an Association would beget social harmony; *Go Ahead!* is their motto!

This proclivity to *Go Ahead!* led to the emergence of many phalanstery communities, many of which comprised only four or five families. These small groups believed that they could achieve social harmony independently of others.

While it may appear obvious to us why these experiments seldom succeeded, I now comprehend that their propagation conformed to the American mindset. Notwithstanding these many failed attempts, the North American Phalanx survived in great measure thanks to its financial capital and its solicitous founders.

At this moment in time, the N.A. Phalanx celebrates ten years of existence. Since its inception, the community has numbered between 120 to 150 members, including women and children. Given that they are so few and that they lack essential theoretical knowledge, notably the awareness that in order to flourish they must increase their numbers, this phalanx was never able to organize its mission within the Process of Series framework. Admittedly, the workshops are structured in groups and units are called series, nevertheless, the work lacks diversity and passion and is performed in a monotone and continuous fashion. At least the operative members are equal, free and remain in partnerships.

To those who are familiar with the phalansterian theory, the North American Phalanx, in its current state, clearly demonstrates the underlying shortcomings that can lead to a group's breakdown; the North American Phalanx has failed to properly apply the Process of Series and all the phenomena intrinsically associated with the proper application of associative rules.

The allure of communal work and the zeal it arouses remain entirely absent. The phalanx notably lacks individual initiative, a quality prevalent in American society, and one that we seek to develop and maintain in our communities. This group seems to vegetate instead of thrive; the members appear bored and apathetic rather than alert, active and impassioned by their work. This clearly points to the improper stimulation of the passions that awaken the Process of Series. We can look at science for proof that emotional investment is key to the success of a collective society; without it, a group will aggregate members whose individuality will dilute itself into a collective subsistence.

On the other hand, the relationship between master and apprentice, landowner and proletariat, powerful entrepreneur and dependent employee; the submissiveness of the salaried worker; the debasement of repulsive jobs; the conflicts and discords caused by lawless competition; the depreciation of salaries; the inferior conditions endured by women, and so on; indeed, all the divisions caused by these situations disappeared and were replaced by equality among workers and among the sexes, the worthiness of labor, the dignity of sensible and consensual subordination, and collective agreement to serve the common interest. It becomes evident that the economic advantages begotten by those who live together in an Association grow proportionally with the number of its members.

Although the organization of the North American Phalanx remains inferior and rudimentary, the group nevertheless succeeds in resolving several social troubles simply by applying, albeit in rudimentary fashion, our principles of Association. As a follower of the phalansterian doctrine,

I experienced deep-felt gratification combined with a certain sadness in regard to the shortcomings directly related to the theoretical practices applied by the members of the North American Phalanx. Yet, a visitor who is uninitiated in the ways of the phalanstery will unconsciously experience a sense of unfamiliar satisfaction when he shares a meal with members of the North American Phalanx. The meals are served by the young sons and daughters as well as the wives of the members of the establishment. They in turn will be served by several members whom they themselves had just served. A visitor experiences nothing less than a great act of accomplished social emancipation: the undertaking of a dignified social function that replaces the subjugation of black slaves and impoverished social outcasts. The visitor bears witness to a successful rehabilitation of human labor, so many acts of which have been debased in our splintered societies. This rehabilitation is indeed a cornerstone of life in our Associations, and visitors can infer this change without needing to understand the theoretical complexities applied to produce this change.

Young girls and women have no problem earning their wages. At a certain age, women take an active role in the decision-making process of the Association; they participate in debates and vote, just like the men. Consequently, social and workplace equality of the sexes is organically established; here again, this simple and natural innovation that most humans who live in society might not ponder, reveals itself to all who visit a Phalanstery Community, thus bearing witness to a great step forward in the history of our human evolution.

The hours not spent on Association tasks are naturally not subject to any type of penalty; there exists no mandatory work schedule and everybody can excuse himself from his tasks at any time; nevertheless, all necessary work is completed in a regular fashion. At the North American Phalanx, one senses no pressure or constraints. One cannot detect even the shadow of an authority figure who reprimands or punishes others; life unfolds in a pleasant and orderly manner and the members' behavior couldn't be any more upstanding or honorable. I imagine that many neighbors looked upon the group with curiosity and some feared that the community might bring pestilence. They were quickly reassured and now live in peaceful harmony alongside the Phalanstery Community.

Every living being lives in some form of Association. The variety and the complexity of tasks along with the degree to which these tasks are organized determine the distinctions among Associations. Within this context, the North American Phalanx of New Jersey can be described as a social zoophyte. This phalanx would require a radical reform in order to elevate itself to a more advanced order, and this would be difficult to accomplish since it has been functioning in this more rudimentary manner for over ten years. Regardless, this Association remains of great value to our organization for we can study the application of our phalansterian theories, thus its members have established their undeniable place in the history of our Social Order. By the by, this group provides valuable insights in regard to our transition procedures, which Brisbane had already described in his report. These observations reveal that the American temperament conforms more easily to the more rudimentary associations. In Europe, our southern populations would not be capable of upholding an association of this type even over the period of fifteen days. The stoic, reserved nature of the Americans, together with their reasonable and detached sociability, enables them to adapt to the changes imposed by their new life, whereas the Europeans remain less audacious about transformation. The careful reflection of this phenomenon captured much of my interest.

III

After six weeks spent gathering invaluable insights among my generous hosts at the North American Phalanx, I left New Jersey, and while I waited for Brisbane to join me at the end of April, I traveled to New York and Boston. Alas, I was still incapable of conversing in English, however, I was able to productively apply the little that I had learned as I spent time in the company of the various friends who supported our cause. I paid a visit to our communities in Lowell and Lawrence (1), two immense centers that grew incredibly rapidly thanks to the practical ingenuity and industriousness of the American people.

Growth in numbers for Lowell and Lawrence:

(1) Population in	1820	1830	1840	1850
Lowell	"	6474	20796	32964
Lawrence	"	"	"	18342

Lawrence in particular encompasses a collection of buildings without equivalent in Europe. The manufactured palaces appear to have sprung from the earth in just a few short years.

I also visited an extremely interesting community, the *Perfectionists*, in Oneida County, and I regret that I was not able to spend more time among them to study their doctrines. Finally, I reached the northern part of New York

State, by the shores of Lake Erie, near Niagara, not far from Batavia, which is where I finally met up with Brisbane. I could digress and include many interesting observations about my experiences during these three months, alas this is not relevant to our objective.

I arrived in America without harboring any preconceived notions of what to expect; my mind was a blank slate. My mission was to inquire, explore and expand my knowledge and to learn all I could about the United States. Inexorably, I found myself prone to examine all of which I came into contact from the point of view of our cause; as a dedicated phalansterian, I carry our cause into all aspects of my life. Furthermore, in America, I encountered like-minded friends who had similarly dedicated their lives to the propagation of our common beliefs. It was only natural that deliberations to establish an Association in America ensued and, in these pages, I will share with you my thoughts that were the fruit of these deliberations.

What particular advantages did America offer? How could our goals be facilitated? These were the hypothetical questions I asked myself during my conversations with our friends and especially with Brisbane who never ceased to believe in our social reforms and dedicated himself to their introduction and their dissemination in America. He came to visit me often during my three months in New York and we regularly engaged in discussions that continued for hours.

During the course of these conversations, we assumed respective roles; Brisbane demonstrated great faith in

America, and he only considered an engagement in his country. For me, on the other hand, America remained merely a hypothetical option since I remained faithful to the idea of an experiment in which the Process of Series would lead to a new harmonious social order. You will discover how we conveniently reached an agreement.

At first, I questioned Brisbane about his ambitious goals, which included the creation of a journal for which he envisioned an extensive readership. Although a journal might find sufficient readership given the expansiveness of America, I believed that the moment for this type of endeavor had passed and that we should concentrate our efforts on the establishment of a transformative society rather than labor to conquer new adherents to our cause. I insisted that we should begin with the conceptualization of a Project for an Association, and we should present our plan through lectures instead of through a time-consuming and binding daily journal.

At the time of my arrival, Brisbane was considering the acquisition of several acres of land in the West (Ohio, Illinois or one of the neighboring states) where we could establish a large-scale operation with great agricultural machines that would rival those used by the firemen in the large Eastern cities. This idea as well as the implied ramifications were quickly abandoned.

At times Brisbane and I would hypothesize how we could take advantage of the North American Phalanx; other times we would discuss how to construct an entire operation to educate potential members based on our European model. We also conferred about a semi-Association paradigm that we encountered in Raritan Bay where there existed a community established by former North American Phalanx members, and also about another group of friends who established an Association in Long Island grounded on the idea of total and absolute individual freedom.

IV

Although our frequent conversations did not lead us to a concrete plan, the myriad ideas which we expounded were far from fruitless. We scrutinized many options and agreed upon some key points. We decided that our project, whatever form it should adhere to, would take on a pragmatic nature; this was a truly pivotal moment in our discussions. Without hesitation, we were in complete accord that our undertaking to create an Association would greatly benefit from the integration of American and European populations. We also agreed to exclude certain geographic areas—Northern, Eastern and what are known as Western States—from our scope for several decisive reasons. First, the long and harsh winters interrupt agricultural life and limit our reliance on nature. This would cause our members to isolate indoors during five, six and up to seven months of time, which would create many inconveniences. These areas are also prone to periods of excessive heat during the summer, and much of the best land has already been appropriated and the remaining parcels demand considerable sums of money. The great valleys of the West, where land is cheaper and climates less extreme, remain nonetheless insalubrious for settlers.

I should like to mention here the recent and remarkable expansion of the Mormons. In a few short years, they have cumulated an astonishing amount of wealth, thanks in part to an unaffectedly socialist solidarity, notwithstanding their retrograde and absurd ideas that include a bizarre mélange of Mohammedanism and patriarchal biblical theocracy. They are on the cusp of constituting a new State, west of the Rocky Mountains. Oh, but the recent foundation of the thirty-two States and Territories that today comprise the American Federation remains genuinely magnificent! This great population of twenty-five million souls saw its beginnings a mere two hundred years ago, thanks to the emigration of a few pilgrims who came to the savage lands of this new continent to seek freedom and flee persecution!

All things considered, Brisbane was inclined to create a community founded on the principle that the State would be a guarantor, which he believed would facilitate its rapid growth. He would frequently state: "If we cannot establish social Harmony, let us at least construct Justice." In our debates, Brisbane remained steadfast in his belief that it would be easier to base an Association on the concepts of Justice rather than on those of social Harmony; I on the other hand maintained that it would be simpler to satisfy our objective by meeting the latter followed by the former instead of trying to achieve both separately. We reached a general accord expressed in this manner: "We seek to create a social environment open to all progressive ideas where those who are loyal to phalanterian principles primarily dedicate themselves to the systematization of *Harmony* as it exists in the Process of Series."

V

I often came back to an initial idea that came to me as I began to hypothesize about an American Association. I contemplated the possibility that there existed vast areas of uninhabited and available tracts of land in the expansive Union territory. One can also assume that the value of the land is determined by the potential density of its population. The ability to bring forth inhabitants to settle particular areas therefore generates the value.

As we know, our members possess a fervent faith in the strength of our Phalanx Communities, therefore, could we not come to America and utilize this virtual capital to establish societies where populations are collectively dedicated to this common objective? This ardent faith could in turn arouse resolute and substantial financial support from our members who might want to participate in the fulfillment of this venture.

Hypothetically, if a considerable portion of our communities from both worlds came together to inhabit an area of hitherto virgin lands, we could swiftly create an independent, financially stable society dedicated to labor and our common values. This idea, which germinated from our personal dictums, became the foundational element of our American Hypothesis. This idea engendered the creation of new roads and means that furthered the conceptualization of our project in the New World, and I fervently believed that this collaborative effort would become indispensable to the success of our future enterprise.

VI

Through our continued discussions, the vagaries our project began to dissipate and a preliminary path emerged. We
initially considered several questions to help us direct our
exploration: Where should we go? What do we seek? What
can we put forward? What are we inclined to risk?

Originally, our indecision compelled us to consider a
course that would take us to the territory beyond the Rocky
Mountains. As I previously mentioned, we eliminated the
lands up North as the climate is harsh and extreme. The rig-
ors of their natural environment command substantial and
arduous labor to ensure survival, and this in turn burdens
and subjugates the proletariat. Instead, more hospitable climates tend to dispose the proletariat toward action; in fact,
these climates escape social afflictions as they oblige passion-
ate labor, which in turn invites the creation of a Harmonious
Social Order. Given these parameters, the Northern winters, the scorching hot summers, the insalubrious nature of
the Western valleys, and the low-lying Southern beaches all
remained outside of our bounds, thus limiting the area of our
research. In short, thanks to detailed information obtained
from the courteous Captain Marcy, who led several explor-
atory missions to the frontier lands of Mexico, we decided
to travel to points closer to the Gulf of Mexico. Indeed, we
intended to begin our journey in Santa Fe, in New Mexico,

in order to explore the area situated at 55 and 56 degrees of latitude, near the Goo-al-pah (the Canadian River) and the Pecos River.

VII

In the past twenty years or so, on numerous occasions, I have had to justify our social experiment to many who insist on drawing connections between it and the matters associated with colonization. I explain that both situations are distinct and encompass considerable struggles, and the attempt to affiliate the two obfuscates their complexities. In America, the risks involved with the equation of our social experiment and colonization took on a concrete nature during my first encounter with the effects of colonization, and this did nothing to assuage my trepidations. I encountered its comprehensive harshness up North in the dense and boggy virgin forest that the pioneers attempted to conquer by fire and by sword. Rudimentary fences separated vast tracts of felled forest; plows had laboriously flattened spaces that remained disseminated with tree stumps so difficult to extract that they remained steadfastly in place, rotted carcasses of their previous majestic selves. From these flat, decrepit landscapes I discerned the willy-nilly outlines of wooden cabins that emerged from the swampy ground, which added to the ambiance of untamable feral disorder. I was not encouraged by these sights.

What were we to encounter in the South? Would the landscapes and nature of this region prove to be as inhospitable as those up North? Extreme heat; fevers; deadly emanations that arise from the ground; the rapid extenuation of strength caused by the heat; a defiant and unyielding forest; the nearby presence of rebellious hordes of Indians; these are the treacherous battlefields that the first generation of settlers encountered.

We soon realized that the forbidding information we heard before embarking on our journey proved to mirror the truth. In fact, there were moments when Brisbane lost all hope, despite his faith in America. On the other hand, I began our trip as a matter of utter curiosity and considered our endeavors with healthy skepticism. Nevertheless, after five months, I was overcome by a deep and compelling emotion: we were living in a land of freedom. Every waking moment, I inhaled freedom from every pore in my body. This freedom was robust, sweeping and as complete as the freedom for Civilization we elaborate in our dreams. This is the freedom that politics alone will never fabricate in Europe. It will forever remain a chimera until we attain our Social Harmony.

I welcomed this liberty and I rejoiced intensely in its existence. I rejoiced at the good it does to the soul and at the dignity it imparts onto a people and how it nurtures human activity and kindles fecund innovations. I witnessed this freedom expressed in a multitude of settings and under many different forms. Freedom is used to conquer Nature; it helps to develop an immense and productive industry; it emboldens prodigious commerce; it influences theories, doctrines and inventions. Everything I encountered radiated freedom, from the air we breathed to the forests and the fields, from the thoughts people expressed to the press they read, from individuals to institutions: everything epitomizes freedom.

This freedom is not a mere element in the fabric of the country, rather, it represents the very essence of the country, its very doctrine. Freedom is the lifeblood, the soul, the dignity, and the reason for which the American people exist. The American people recognize that they presently represent Freedom to the entire world and that they have become the custodians of this Freedom for humanity's foreseeable future.

The actions that result from this freedom are not merely a right, they also represent an honor. Americans are instinctively aware of the complications begotten by innovation; however, rather than curtail novelty, they not only welcome it, they encourage it as well as the inevitable failures that oftentimes ensue. In America, a fall simply proves that one can walk, and Americans cherish all who are capable of walking! Go ahead! This is their motto. Not a thing that falls down honorably is trodden.

American is currently the World's Homeland of Creativity. She is essentially a champion of diversity, of action, of enterprise, indeed of adventure. This represents the exact opposite of our aging Europe, who remains timorous, predictable even in its more progressive endeavors, despotic even in its ideas about freedom. Oh, my friends! What a grand and powerful ideal is liberty! How nourishing is its breath and how fortifying the delight it incites! If only Europe offered similar circumstances, or perhaps if our European followers were in America, how quickly we would attain our purpose! Even though I entertained these hypotheses, I confess that I found them both equally illusive. I pondered how to properly express, in spoken or even in written words, the full and vertiginous force of the emotions that I experienced. How could I rupture deep-rooted habits and conquer inherent inertia? How could I rouse the torpid and help them triumph over prejudice and their fear of the unknown, and arouse a collective and even reckless determination among our members?

With the writing of these words, I endeavored to describe to you my thoughts and my frame of mind. You have here, my friends, a perfunctory vision of my mindset at the time.

VIII

On April 30, Brisbane and I were finally able to leave the shores of Lake Erie where giant ice masses still floated on the frigid water. Even the shrubs remained steadfastly bare, without the slightest hint of swelling buds on their bare branches. We were going to Texas and planned our approach from the north, by the Red River, but first we would travel on the Ohio River, the Mississippi and through parts of Arkansas. The first day we found ourselves southwest of Cleveland and the next day, we continued to travel south toward Wellsville, Ohio. The following day we arrived in Canton where we were greeted by friends of our Cause. On April 30 we had left behind the fullness of winter in Buffalo, but in Canton, located only two degrees south, we stepped into spring! The invigorating temperature offset the warmth of the sun, colorful flowers blossomed in gardens, and the birds were in the throes of lust and labor, the ardor of which I had never before witnessed in Europe. I will never forget the appeal of this magnificent change of scenery.

I noted that in this area the oeuvre of colonization had been much less exacting. The landscape was more prairie than forest and the undulating terrain supported a variety of agriculture. Woodlands skirted the plateaus, and the streams and lakes, lined with majestic trees, all melded into a vibrant and jubilant landscape.

On the afternoon of May 2, we reached Cincinnati by

travelling through the foothills of the Allegheny Mountains. Our destination was a place called Patriot where we would visit some very dear friends of our Cause. We were greeted with open arms. We shared our purpose, and they enthusiastically agreed with our mission to find a site on virgin lands. I can still hear Allan: "Find what is most suitable and in eight days I will sell my land and settle my affairs, and I will be ready to join you."

In Cincinnati, we also planned to meet my old friend, Gingembre, who lived on the outskirts of the city, on the banks of the Ohio River, where he had built a small house, in only eight days, with the help of his two sons. Disheartened with Europe, Gingembre left with his family toward the end of 1849 and, like the majority of those who left Europe for America, he continuously commended his decision. He repeatedly encouraged us to convince all of our friends to leave Europe to come to America where together we could accomplish great feats. His three children had successfully settled down. It must be noted that they all spoke English before their arrival.

During our visit in this prosperous and thriving city, I gave further thought to one of my preoccupations, the question of the material challenges involved in establishing a settlement. I contemplated the arsenal needed to settle a country's interior lands. In America, the tools used in the battle to conquer nature are organized like an army at war organizes the equipment needed by its offensive forces. All that is necessary is stored and maintained in repositories and various types of storage facilities. The operations conducted have become so predictable that the process of land settlement operates like a manufacturing business. The tools, the procedures and the implementation are so structured that it is similar to the production of hats, or fabric or even wood boards. If the practice of land settlement elsewhere is plagued with troubles, then it appears that in America it has been efficiently and decisively resolved.

Even though this issue appeared to be sorted out, other doubts percolated in my mind, such as the procurement and cost of land parcels in the Western regions favored by Brisbane. Nevertheless, as we traveled further West, our familiarity with these lands increased and our knowledge developed.

IX

When we left Patriot, we bade farewell to the last friends that we would encounter during our journey. We had few supplies as we traveled through the forests and prairies of the Indian Territories toward Texas. We distanced ourselves from the peaks of Allegheny as we followed the Ohio River toward the endless plains of the Mississippi basin. What openness! We began our course in the great state of Ohio and followed the borders of the states of Indiana, Illinois, Missouri and Arkansas on our right, and Kentucky, Tennessee, and Mississippi on our left. Good Lord, what spaciousness! and what a magnificent future awaits this great Federation of magnificent open spaces, interspersed with flourishing cities, that extend from whence the sun rises to where it sets. Oh, great Union, we beseech that you grow and proliferate! You are already the great motherland of Democracy, of labor, and of all the elements that fashion the modern world. Whatever happens, you are destined to become the sanctuary of its most progressive ideas and their implementation.

When we reached the Mississippi, we sailed down the majestic waterway, steam flowing from its ships day and night. The vastness of the river made it feel as though we were travelling on the ocean. We were cradled between the blue sky, the forceful, grayish waters and the extravagant vegetation that extends infinitely along the riverbanks. Once we reached Arkansas, we traveled up the Arkansas River to Little Rock, in the center of the state, named after this waterway. We delighted in the landscape's shift from interminable vistas of water toward scenes of rocky terrain laced with undulating hills.

According to Captain Marcy, we were to purchase horses in Little Rock and then head toward Preston, the last inhabited point in Texas along the Red River. We quickly learned that a stagecoach traveled this route weekly. We also discovered that a steamboat regularly navigated the Red River between Little Rock and Fort Smith, the westernmost civilized point of the Union that bordered on Indian Territories extending all the way to the Rocky Mountains. We momentarily considered this detour, however, we quickly decided to continue along our agreed route.

The pitch slowly rose along the banks of the river and hills rose along the horizon. When we stopped for a few hours in Van Buren, we encountered red-skinned Osage Indians and were struck by their remarkable beauty; they would remain the most impressive indigenous peoples we encountered. We continued to travel further and further from civilization; our trip was becoming a genuine expedition. With our new horses and up-to-date information, on the afternoon of May 19, we crossed the Poteau River on a barge crafted from tree trunks and headed toward the territory of the Choctaw Indians. The French adventurers who named the river were the first white men to hunt along its shores.

The regions through which we traveled in one day's time could not have diverged more brusquely. We began in Fort Smith, a settlement dotted with white and red brick houses, separated by colorful gardens, set along wide, straight roads where women in muslin dresses walked in and out of stores that sold a myriad of goods. This town was home to young and prosperous professionals such as lawyers, doctors, jewelers, and watchmakers, and it harbored several large steamboats that sailed up and down the Arkansas River.

Less than two hours from this bustling port, we were leading our horses, with great difficulty, through a swampy forest whose thick canopy obstructed the sunlight so effectively that we felt as though we were travelling in middle of the night. The somber solitude; the silence; the pungent odors; the luxuriant vegetation; the gigantic vines entangled in the trees; the accumulated vestiges of ancient wildlife: alone with these elements, we experienced the full impact of nature's pureness and understood the untamed energy of *natura naturans*. It was superb!

By nightfall, we entered the village of Choctawa, an Indian village where we stopped to eat. We were served by a dark-skinned female slave who brought us hot bread, raw onions, and a plate with a flat, burned piece of food that I initially thought was a carbonized piece of meat. To my surprise, when I bit into it, I discovered that I had been served a deliciously prepared fish: the exterior char protected the delicate, raw flesh.

In the forest, we encountered only a few wild boars and

three drunk Indians on horseback. This was the only village we found in this Indian Territory until we reached the border of Texas, and it afforded us a brief view of the difficult transition from uncivilized to civilized society. In these peripheral areas, black people enslaved by the Redskins become their teacher and introduce the Indians to agriculture, industry and even music. During the night, while we tried to sleep, we could hear strange musical sounds from the surrounding log cabins, but we were hard pressed to identify what instruments were being played. I would like to elaborate my thoughts regarding this transferral of subservience, however, I must remind myself again that my writings must not stray from my strict objective.

We left Choctawa and made our way to the home of an Indian of mixed race, since we were told that this was a suitable place to stop for the night. Once we stopped, I was overtaken by a strong fatigue and I soon realized that I had a fever. That night, the persistent fever robbed me of sleep and that morning I did not have the strength to rise. Later that day, three Americans arrived on horseback and they told us that recent rains had caused the surrounding rivers to overflow, and they were forced to swim across three of them. I had heard many disturbing stories about the dangerous illnesses one could encounter in the Southwest. This physical setback prompted all sorts of doubts about our expedition and my ability to pursue this endeavor. I imagined myself stranded in these woods, deprived of all assistance, unable to move forward or to go back.

Thankfully Brisbane was in fine health and he took control of the situation with his strong American confidence. He deduced that my afflictions were most likely caused by the rapid and abrupt changes I experienced, together with my physical fatigue from days on horseback (I had not ridden in over twenty years!). He suggested we try to forge ahead and believed that resuming our journey might produce some homeopathic effects. Brisbane was right: after only a few miles, my health and demeanor began to improve. That night, we ate with an Indian who had killed a wild turkey, and after a few bites of the roasted meat, I began to regain my appetite and my strength. I mention this incident to show that one need not become discouraged or sidetracked by inconveniences. Further, it is a reminder to myself that up until that moment, I had not yet fully embraced the purpose of our expedition; however, this incident marked the turning point in my purpose, when I became fully aware that nothing could deter my faith and commitment in leading a successful expedition for our cause.

X

By the middle of the fourth day our surroundings began to transform, and we were allured by scenes of arresting beauty. Until then, the nature before us remained harsh and inhospitable, with impenetrable forests, riverbanks encased by insurmountable knolls of mud and a constrained horizon. The earth was no doubt fertile, but what formidable toil was required to tame it!

After almost five hours of travel on the fourth day, the tall grasses of a great valley swayed before us and the combined sunlight and wind bequeathed the landscape an ethereal quality. From right to left, the luxuriant prairie gracefully undulated below us as it extended toward verdant forests that clambered up the slopes of the surrounding mountains. A floral symphony blanketed the velvet grasses of the vales that encircled us; the prairies diffused along the edges of the forest that protruded from the swards like isthmus and capes. A willy-nilly assemblage of oak, elm, hickory, and walnut trees festooned the slopes while colorful and sinuous vegetation rambled along the creeks.

In all my American travels, I had never encountered a landscape with as much appeal as the scene before me at the Red River Basin. Brisbane and I were both struck by its simultaneously untamed yet manicured demeanor. Imagine for a moment the gardens of Windsor and Richmond, and replace the fog with the radiant sunshine of a southern sky. This image might at least convey the panorama that unfolded before us; however, our eyes would encounter nary a castle nor a luxurious residence that frequently intersperse the orchards and pastures of Europe.

Nature has done everything: everything is ready, everything is in place, except for the structures. Nothing claimed, none of the land has been parceled; there are no impediments. What a formidable theater from whence to launch our operation. This could become the birthplace of Harmony! Boundless new ideas and prospects unfolded before me. Brisbane had already been confirmed in his faith for America; I was experiencing my baptism.

We began to envision the prospect of our destiny of open, communal, and harmonious labor unfold within the confines of the seemingly inviting nature of our majestic surroundings. All the necessary elements were present: the climate, the open sky, the fertile soil, the expansiveness, the bounty! In contrast, reflect on the state of our own gangrenous world beset by declining civilizations, riddled with vice, controlled by interests and overrun by despotism, war and revolutions. Faced with these inescapable realities, I ask you, how can we not view our departure for America as our Providential destiny? How can the desire to go there and preserve our progressive ideas for humankind not irrupt within your soul? I, myself, witnessed the light of the burning bush, and my eyes have been opened to the reality of our future. Brisbane of course needed no convincing; nevertheless, I still needed to better understand the different facets of our undertaking before I could expunge any latent hesitations.

XI

All Indian territory was unavailable as it was set aside for the tribal peoples, rightfully so. According to federal law, a white person could settle on their lands only through marriage. Simple wooden fences served as the only physical and legal demarcations of properties. It remained to be seen if in Texas the laws were as straightforward and as attractive, as this would greatly facilitate the establishment of a settlement, which was rapidly moving from the realm of theoretical impression toward the domain of actual realism.

The last detail I will mention about this part of our trip involves our encounter with a German settler who shared valued information regarding the climate, the soil and the conditions of the area. Within six years, this man transformed these primitive surroundings into a thriving farm with cultivated fields, cattle, gardens, and orchards. The Peutcher family's farmed oasis emphatically proved to us that it would be possible to coax a successful settlement out of these environments, particularly if we prepared ourselves properly. What could we expect from Texas?

As we approached the Red River, our encounters with settlers became more frequent. Everybody seemed to agree that the Indian Territories did not pose any threat and that Texas was a hospitable land. Once again doubts invaded my mind as we faced the physical immensity of the space before us as well as the intricacies of the task that lay ahead. It would be necessary for myriad elements to align in order for our project to succeed, and its inception rested upon my ability to convey the sweeping opportunities that await us and to awaken in you, my fellow members, an unbridled need to collectively converge upon this cause.

I carried the burden of these uncertainties with me as we began our eighth day of travel since leaving Fort Smith. We began to notice flickers of gold and red through the fissures in the dense foliage along our path. Soon we found ourselves in the town of Preston, along the banks of the Red River. We had finally entered Texas!

My friends, I have summarily described our journey thus far in an effort to convey the evolution of my thoughts so you can better comprehend how I arrived at the conclusions that I will elaborate in my report. In the next chapters, I will focus on the details of our stay in Texas, the period between May 27 and July 10. During these six weeks, we traveled south of the Red River, toward the Trinity and the Brazos. We sailed down the Colorado River to the city of Austin. We crossed over the Brazos River again as we traveled south to the Bay of Galveston, where the diaphanous waters of the bay swell with the currents of the Gulf Stream that escapes through the Old Bahama Channel. We left Texas via New Orleans, where we were detained for two weeks because of a yellow fever epidemic that had just erupted when we arrived. I reached New York on August 5, after a short stop in Havana. I finally landed in Ostend nine months after I set sail from Antwerp. Now, let us concentrate on our time in Texas.

PART TWO

IN TEXAS

I

The State of Texas is roughly the same size as France, about two hundred thousand square miles. Its boundaries extend from the Gulf of Mexico to the Rio Grande River up to the Sabine River. In the western part of the State, mountains separate Texas from New Mexico, and the Red River runs along its north and northeast border.

Vast low-lying alluvial plains edge the regions along the gulf. Bays and lagoons extend along the coast and the dense vegetation that grows within these areas interrupts the inland course of the gulf. The lands from the coastal area begin a gradual rise from the southeast toward the northwest where elevated plateaus form the foothills of the Guadalupe Mountains.

Texas' abundant waterways serve as the State's prodigious natural irrigation system. All the main waterways flow parallel from the northwestern part of the state down toward the southeast. On a map, one can recognize the tributaries and their myriad transversal offshoots that ripple through the valleys toward the sea.

As you make your way north, away from the low-lying plains, gentle hills begin to rise and they bisect the valleys, although these remain wide open spaces. The surface of these great plains undulates like ocean waves that have quelled after a storm. We were told that up toward the Red River, around the source of the Trinity, the elevation reached eight hundred to nine hundred meters above sea level, but I wonder if this measurement is slightly exaggerated.

An immense forest, called the Cross Timbers, extends throughout the little-known region northeast of the Red River. Great rolling prairies, traversed by countless streams, intersect the forest. The richness of the soil sustains luxuriant vegetation, the likes of which we can scarcely imagine in Europe. One also encounters more arid and rocky spaces within the Cross Timbers. These expanses, interspersed solely by post oak trees, are easily traversed on horseback. These areas are regularly cleared by fires that burn saplings and other varieties of undergrowth; only the solitary and robust post oak survives. Along the borders of the streams, lush vegetation grows indiscriminately, indifferent to the perils of the blazes.

I cannot exactly recall the preconceived idea I gave thought to regarding this prairie, but I am fairly certain that I expected to find unyielding wilderness. To my surprise, this Texas prairie, thanks to the superior quality of its soil, produces magnificent pastureland, with an abundant variety of lush grasses such as wild wheat, oats, and barley. The stalks grew so compactly and so tall that I was reminded of our fallow land back home. I unfortunately lost all the samples that I had collected.

We concluded that the prairie land was in general highly fertile and thrived thanks to the regular forest fires that I previously mentioned. Without these blazes, the forest would overrun the prairies. The practice of controlled blazes was adopted by settlers who, in an effort to maintain and expand the arable land, synchronize and control periodic fires.

You are now familiar with the general configuration of the Texas land and the principal forms of vegetation that grow in the state. To the north and the center, you have the rolling prairies and the post oak forests; toward the west, the terrain becomes increasingly hilly; toward the south, one encounters vast plains and quasi tropical growth. During our travels, we only skirted the westernmost part of the state, where the hills give way to actual mountains. The scenery was splendid albeit deserted as the Native Indians were recently displaced from these lands and the white settlers have not yet arrived.

During the first eleven days of our journey, we were accompanied by a small garrison from Fort Worth; our group encountered nary a human figure nor any trace of a settlement. We came across an abundance of wild turkeys, antelope, and deer, and for this we were grateful as they provided ample and satisfying nourishment.

After only a few short days in Texas, we became convinced that its land beckoned us to settle upon its fertile soil. The information we gathered during our exploration as well

as our careful study of the nature of our surroundings confirmed that we should heed our instincts. Upon reading my
report, in which I describe the elements as well as the economic and social characteristics of the State of Texas, you
too shall become convinced that this state represents the
most ideal location for our future settlement.

II

We discovered that the accounts we heard about Texas' fertile lands were in no way overstated. It is widely recognized that none of the existing thirty-two states have as high a percentage of productive arable lands as Texas. I daresay that even the lands that are considered uncultivable are simply misunderstood; many of these zones would make excellent vineyards. Americans don't seem to have any understanding of wine growing, therefore none of the current settlers realize that certain grapes thrive on rocky hills. They disdain any land that is not suitable for growing cereal, cotton or sugar cane. Yet nature reveals its plans: we encountered an abundance of undomesticated vines that produce clusters of edible black grapes, roughly the size of cherries, and ripe for picking in June. We discovered that one of our compatriots in Dallas, the fearless Gouhénans (a disciple of Étienne Cabet and the leader of the first group of settlers of New Icaria, Iowa, a nineteenth-century utopian community), harvested the grapes and made wine, which he sold for one dollar (five francs) a bottle. I have no doubt that these rocky hills can be transformed into first-rate vineyards.

As for the arable lands and alluvial plains that cover much of the state, we identified four principal categories of soil: black sandy soil; red sandy soil; mulatto soil; and black sticky soil, found mainly close to waterways. All four types of soil are exceedingly fertile, in particular the black sticky soil that is ideal for growing cotton.

It is rather simple to clear the land to ready it for cultivation, even the areas of black sticky soil. Once an area is ploughed and aerated, the seeds can be planted and tended. This suffices to produce cornstalks that measure two to three meters in height and yield an abundant harvest. The corn bears twenty-five, thirty, forty, and even up to forty-five ears per seed. On plots that had been cultivated for only two years, and were not considered to be of highest quality, we found beets that measured almost eighty-two centimeters in circumference!

It is worth noting that all this farming is achieved without the use of manure, which represents an essential base for our European agriculture. In Texas, the soil itself generates its own fertilizers as it is covered by a layer of humus that can measure up to five meters in depth in the areas where black sticky soil is present. Even in the areas where the rich humus in not present, the mineral elements in the alluvial soil are so prolific that it is possible to maintain dynamic and plentiful growth. Realize that I am limiting my comments to what I observed, and I do not endeavor to persistently expound justifications.

You now understand how easily the Texas prairie can be transformed into farmland; this land is equally well suited for gardening. Near Fort Worth and Fort Graham, we found numerous gardens, adjacent to the homes of soldiers, that produced a wide assortment of fruits and vegetables: many varieties of beans; sweet peas; melons; sweet potatoes; all types of plants with which we were not familiar; and row and rows of tomatoes, since these are extensively consumed in America. The most astounding element was that none of these gardens are irrigated, weeded nor tended to in any sort of fashion! We couldn't believe our eyes!

It is natural to expect weeds to grow in areas such as these, but nobody could explain to us why, once the gardens were planted, no weeds appeared, even though we were in mid-June. If I were not addressing this report to friends, I wouldn't dare mention these particularities for fear that my readers would accuse me of reciting tales. Nonetheless, we not only witnessed firsthand all that I relate to you, we also gathered ample information on every matter. We also interrogated dozens of people, including soldiers, farmers, tradesmen, and even Indians, and they all affirmed our knowledge.

Since the harvest ends on May 25 (when it extends to the beginning of June it is considered delayed), we asked if they usually planned two harvests. They responded that they had no need to do this since the single harvest produces an abundance of crop.

I believe that I have written enough about the characteristics of the soil and the general agricultural conditions. One addition detail that I would like to commit to paper is the nature of the rocky terrain that surrounds the great valleys: it is mostly calcareous but at times consists of sandstone.

We found rock-hard coal in the Indian Territories and in the upper regions of Texas. Iron abounds and, scattered throughout the state, one finds the remains of pelagic shells, horns of Ammon as well as belemnites. The Western regions contain rich deposits of various types of metals and I recognized large gypsum deposits similar to those of the Parisian quarries. Indeed, entire basins rest upon deep layers of metallic marl, which produce dirt that is easy to dig and soft when extracted but hardens as soon as it is exposed to air.

I gathered many soil samples in order to have them analyzed, but unfortunately, I lost them all. I am certain that we would have found them to contain an extensive variety of elements.

III

The richness of a country's soil can be appraised and agricultural production can be estimated. Climate is entirely different: its impact causes suffering or delight. A benevolent climate enhances every aspect of life. In this next chapter, I hope to describe the Texas climate as accurately as possible. I will focus specifically on the area located around the thirty-third and thirty-fourth degrees of latitude, in the northern part of the state. I'm certain you are aware that these latitudes, the same at which the island of Madeira is situated, represent the most favored latitudes on earth as they are not subject to the extreme weather one encounters closer to the equator or at the northern and southern poles. Three elements combine to create a perfect climate in this degree of latitude: the specific temperatures on the American continent; the elevation of the land masses; and the atmosphere's undercurrents.

In Europe, the hot summer temperatures around the thirty-third and thirty-fourth degree parallels would make acclimating difficult for the populations coming from the north, especially during the initial phases when we establish a settlement. Nonetheless, it is a well-known fact that, generally speaking, the temperatures at those very same parallels in the New World are considerably less harsh than those in Europe. Winters in New York, situated at the same longitude as Naples, are longer and harsher than those in Paris, and the tropical heat in America is far less intense than that in Africa. It is estimated that there is a roughly six-degree difference in the temperatures at the same latitudes.

The prevailing wind in Texas comes from the south, from the Gulf of Mexico. The breeze blows roughly between seven in the morning and four or five in the afternoon. Occasionally, the wind comes from the north, and rarely it blows from the east or the west.

The land mass slopes gently toward the Gulf and the elevation around the forks of the Trinity River rises to roughly eight hundred to nine hundred meters above sea level. You can now easily imagine the magnificence of the climate in North Texas that results from the confluence of its latitude, the specificities of the climate on the American continent, the continuous southern breeze, the region's elevation, and the southeastern exposure of the great valley that shelter it from the northerly winter wind.

The latitude protects the area against harsh winters and allows cacti, mimosas, and other delicate vegetation to flourish. The altitude also favors agriculture and all of the crops with which we are familiar in Europe grow splendidly in this area. The one aspect of the climate that I cannot justly describe is the flowing southern breeze that envelops the region like a silk sheath. To experience its velvety touch is to understand both its gentleness and its vigor. I dare say that this breeze is indeed the crowning glory of Texas' natural cornucopia! It tempers the heat in the valleys and plateaus, thus making it possible for men to ride their horses at midday, during June and July. It attenuates the cold from north so winter temperatures generally only last for no more than three consecutive days, and the sixty-odd days of winter resemble our nicest days in May. This breeze brings with it the rains that sustain the crops and fill the waterways that shape Texas' superb natural irrigation system.

Regarding the seasons, winter begins during the latter half of November when the northern winds begin to blow intermittently, but never for more than two or three days. If ever snow falls during the night, it disappears by early afternoon. There are generally no more than thirty cold days per winter; the remaining sixty are temperate and delightful, thanks to Gulf breeze. Be warned that during this season, the changes in temperature can be abrupt and unpredictable, so it is best to dress accordingly.

In conclusion, winter in northern Texas is a true fillip, bolstering men and nature alike. In a more practical sense, it also allows the settlers to harvest ice for use during the summer months, a very common practice among Americans. Also, one need not invest much money in a winter wardrobe as one can sport summer clothes during two thirds of the winter season. The commanding office in Fort Worth told us that during this past winter, he led several expeditions into the Texas wilderness, some lasting up to two full weeks, and the nights were so mild that he and his men would often forgo setting up tents for the night.

By mid-February, nature awakens, and by the beginning of March, it gains full consciousness. As I previously mentioned, by May 25, the harvest was complete, and by the end of June, while cotton plants bloomed, we picked ripe wild plums and grapes, ate seasoned watermelon, and roasted or boiled maize that was served at many meals. In June and July, the sun appeared to be ten degrees from its zenith, but my straw hat provided sufficient relief from its hot rays. In fact, I found the heat in New York and in New Orleans to be far more difficult to tolerate.

The settlers in Texas come from all corners of the Union, with the majority principally from the neighboring Western and Southern States; however, we also met settlers who came from the North. The Union soldiers we encountered originated from a wide variety of countries: Ireland, France, England, and Spain. We even met soldiers from Russia and Sweden! In all my travels in Europe and in America, I invariably encountered residents who complained about their locale's weather—except in Texas where all we heard from the inhabitants was a continuous litany of praise for what they considered to be the best place in the world to live. The refrains we heard countless times when we asked locals to share their impressions of North Texas were all similarly enthusiastic: "It's the greatest land and the most wonderful climate in the world!"; "The finest country of all the United States!"; "The finest climate in the world!"

I struggle to describe the serenity and genial atmosphere of the summer evenings we spent in Texas: the air, the warmth, the earth, and the sky amalgamate to form a perfectly harmonious cocoon. These moments, so rarely experienced in our countries back home, lulled our very souls into a state of utter bliss. To ignite their inspiration, our poets chase these moments along the shores of the Gulf of Naples or by the Adriatic, whereas almost every evening, the Texas sunsets beacon unbounded inspiration.

In short, the winter brings generally thirty or so days of cold weather (not nearly as harsh as what we are used to), and the summer sees an occasional day where the heat of the sun triumphs over all other elements; such are the exceptions in the otherwise perfect climate of these North Texas counties. Regarding the rain, Texas does have a rainy season as it exists in tropical countries. The rain in Texas is spread fairly evenly throughout the year and it comes in intervals that last between six and twelve days. Some summers can be dry; however, the vegetation does not appear to suffer from this as the soil retains enough moisture to sustain the plants during these periods. Wells are generally fifteen to twenty feet deep and are able to provide water throughout the year.

I must include two more observations before concluding this chapter about the climate. You will quickly appreciate the importance of the first actuality as it directly impacts agricultural expenditures: shelters for domestic animals are nowhere to be found. Cattle, horses and hogs roam and graze freely year-round throughout the woods and the prairies. Even in the winter, the settlers do not provide any fodder for their animals. Nature provides for all their needs. The result of this extraordinary arrangement is the most superb looking livestock I have ever seen. Only in Switzerland does one see such handsome cattle. Livestock farming in Texas consists of branding the animals and letting them wander about freely. This is what a settler explained: "You see these animals? They cost us less to raise than our chickens cost us to maintain. We have to build sheds for our poultry otherwise they will escape, and we feed them grains. Our cattle feed off the prairie. When the herd wanders off, one of the children sets off on horseback to bring them closer. Once in a while, we gather the young ones to brand them, otherwise, the cattle don't cause us any problems and we have no expenses."

The second practicality relates to the dwellings of the settlers themselves. When a new settler arrives on his land, he and his family set up a makeshift camp while he cuts his timbers to build a home. Once he has gathered all the wood he needs, his neighbors (some can live six to ten miles away) arrive on horseback with tools and food. The new settler shares his design with the men and together they build the dwelling. Most settlers consider these log cabins a temporary home; nevertheless, thanks to the mild climate, they become the permanent homes for the majority of the settlers, hence the temporary becomes permanent. I'm certain you can anticipate the ease with which one can build a settlement in this environment. Aside from the proper tools, one need only supply a good amount of elbow grease to construct these tasteful and practical homes, so well suited to the Texas climate. Let us now move to another topic.

IV

One of the most pressing issues we investigated with the utmost solicitude concerns the salubriousness of the area in which we are interested. We gathered a considerable amount of information about this matter, and we can summarize it by stating, very simply, that all the plains, plateaus and open valleys pose no health concerns whatsoever, whereas the marshy areas adjacent to the woodlands can incite fevers during the summer months. During our travels, this modest rule allowed us to anticipate the health conditions of any settlement we visited. Given the reliability of these observations, we were surprised by many setters' imprudence and ignorance when choosing a location to build their dwellings.

We ascertained that any settlement removed from the flatlands close to the sea would remain most healthy for the inhabitants. Aside from the seasonal fevers due mostly to the occasional, sudden fluctuations in temperatures in the winter, there exist no health risks in this area of Texas. In fact, we spoke with doctors and soldiers, and also consulted hospital records. The conversations we had and the facts we checked all confirm that the healthfulness of North Texas remains as fortuitous as the region's climate and its fruitfulness.

Of course, the soldiers' living conditions inside the forts are not the most sanitary: periods of idleness are abruptly interrupted by three to four week-long expeditions in the woodlands where soldiers bivouac near available sources of water. Even though these conditions are not the most ideal, the military doctors with whom we spoke assured us that the general health of the soldiers in Texas was the best when compared to all the other troops in the United States.

We concluded that once the settlers in this region fabricate more comfortable dwellings and develop a more cultured social life, people from all over the Union will flock to this area in order to enjoy its rich health benefits, just as Europeans travel to the Hyères Islands, Nice and to certain parts of Italy.

V

So far, I have sketched the geography, the agricultural richness, the climate, and the salubriousness of our area of interest. For purposes of credibility, I wish I could add additional features that would detract from this area's appeal; however, to do so would be deceitful. Brisbane and I went to many lengths to find hidden foes, but we were unable to expose any negative elements, other than those which I already described. The mosquitoes that abound near the beaches in the southern parts of the State remain insignificant up north, so much so that I remember being more bothered by these pests during the summer in Paris, and I was certainly tormented by them during my stay in New Orleans. Horseflies disturbed our horses only during thirty-six hours at the end of May while we traveled through the Cross Timbers. Other animals, such as rattlesnakes, prairie dogs and buffalo, quickly retreat once settlers arrive. Wild hogs appear to be less common in Texas than in the Northern and Eastern United States. Indeed, Brisbane assured me that he encountered fewer rattlesnakes during his morning walks in Texas than he did when, as a youth, he walked along the shores of the Niagara River. Wild animals are inexistent; wolves attacked only sheep and wild pigs, never horses or cattle as happens in Europe. Bears are hunted for their pelts and for their meat and the woodlands teem with excellent game. The biggest inconvenience we discovered, not only in

Texas, was an abundance of ants whose mounds are easily destroyed.

I suppose the regular prairie fires naturally cull the rattlesnake population and the almost constant breezes help to limit the presence of insects. The mention of insects reminds me that we noticed an abundance of mulberry trees that could be ideal for the cultivation of silkworms. The mention of these trees in turn reminds me of the magnificent magnolia trees, as tall as oaks, that abound in this region.

I can safely state, without fear of being refuted, that Texas is the crown jewel of the Union's thirty-two states, and its northern counties are among the most favored lands in the world. I doubt that similar areas in Mexico, Brazil or Spain offer such rich and diverse natural surroundings. In addition, the political, social and industrial climates in those countries remain far less favorable to the establishment and development of settlements.

Now that I have outlined the major physical attributes of our area of interest, I can begin to clarify the economic and social conditions. I will describe these in no particular order; nevertheless, I will strive to contextualize and explain these circumstances to the best of my ability.

VI

Texas is a newly established State. During the first part of this century, the area was part of the Mexican Empire. Texas became independent in 1836 and joined the Union in 1845. During the Mexican presence, the northern areas of Texas remained rather deserted, and only the coastal lands were occupied by Spanish speakers. Eventually, the regions along the borders of Louisiana and Arkansas were settled by Anglo-Americans, and, as their numbers increased, they cast aside the Mexican yoke. In the interior, toward the forests and prairies, herds of buffalo roamed freely and the native Indian populations followed in their paths. When we traveled along the western fork of the Trinity River, our horses often navigated the trails these herds cleared through the deep ravines in the woods. So much of America's most beautiful landscapes remain wild and uninhabited.

The settlement of Texas began in the coastal areas and expanded toward the Eastern border by Louisiana and up toward Arkansas, itself a recent member of the Union. The population then spread north and northeast along the rivers and spilled into the valleys. Most settlers came to Texas from neighboring States and even today, Texas remains relatively unfamiliar to many of the inhabitants of the Eastern and Northern United States.

All those who arrive in Texas seem to have one thing in common: they arrive with nothing—or close to nothing.

We asked hundreds of people and they all told a similar story, the same tale we had already heard from the German settler, Mr. Putcher. One person arrived with his family, a wagon, a couple of horses and five dollars; another came with only two oxen; another arrived with nothing at all. These were the stories we heard again and again. Yet, after a certain number of years, these same families owned cattle, horses, and hogs; they farmed land that produced an abundance of wheat, potatoes, and corn; they raised chickens and tended lush vegetable gardens.

We witnessed settlers, who arrived without a single possession, work to earn two steer and some seeds. Three months later these same men would begin their own enterprises. We saw a man, who five years ago had but one cow, establish a herd and farm his land in order to feed and raise a family of twelve. We learned of countless similar stories. A young French artisan arrived two years ago in the area of the upper Trinity River with only a dollar in his pocket. He is now the owner of the nicest workshop in Dallas, which he built with his own money. Bourgeois, a French tailor who settled in Dallas, told us that in one day he earns enough to cover his weekly expenses. He was awarded first place in a sewing contest for an overcoat, and his prize was a pregnant sow. Thanks to the offspring produced by the animal, he fed his family for two years, and then he sold the remaining herd to his neighbor for the sum of eighty dollars, or four hundred francs.

I realize that all this can seem extraordinary; however, if

I were to recount all the stories of this nature that we came across, all the pages in this report would not suffice. The stories are in fact so similar that the details all blend together and become intertwined in my memory. At first, we could not believe that this state of affairs was possible. For instance, when I asked how could it be that horses, hogs, and cattle, that cost nothing to feed and raise, could maintain their market value, people responded: "It is just so, and we do not ask ourselves why it is this way." Naturally, I deliberated the causes of these circumstances and determined that several factors contributed to this environment: the progressive and constant arrival of new populations; the accessibility of transportation; and the great value placed on work. These factors are particularly entrenched and dominant in Texas.

The new arrivals benefit from the bountiful natural resources simply by establishing a homestead. Within ten years, settlers, who often arrive with nothing, become rich, sometimes very rich! For example, in Austin, plots that sold for five dollars five years ago now demand six thousand dollars each. We heard of a cobbler, whose net worth was zero dollars when he arrived, amass a fortune worth millions of dollars. Opportunities abound particularly in Galveston where people's fortunes have increased proportionally to the population.

VII

It is difficult for Europeans to grasp the rapidity of growth and therefore activity that propels American society. This progress in turn allows its population to develop staggering wealth, almost as if it were a fairy tale. In 1830, New York's population of roughly two hundred thousand souls lived mostly in dwellings constructed mostly out of wood. Not so today! New York's population in 1850 was at about five hundred fifteen thousand, and New York measured a league in length and continues to expand. Marble and granite mansions line entire city avenues; dazzling luxury and riches of all sorts skirt the entire span of Broadway, the city's central road. The land surrounding New York Harbor was scarcely inhabited twenty years ago, and now dwellings extend as far as the eye can see. Brooklyn counted around twelve thousand in 1830, and now there are more than one hundred thousand residents. A profusion of villas and country homes enshrouds Staten Island, an area that remained unoccupied thirty years ago.

New York's transformation occurs so rapidly that if one is absent for only a few months, it becomes impossible to recognize entire areas of the city as myriad edifices replace swaths of previously empty terrains. A French man who lived in New York for twenty years recounted that, for many years, he had hunted wild duck in the heart of the city, along Canal Street, an area now lined with buildings and no longer considered central as the city continues its precipitous expansion north.

Whilst I visited Buffalo, Brisbane showed me a plot of land that one of his father's friends had gifted him when he was fourteen or fifteen years old. The man told Brisbane that the lot was of little value, but, in due time, the land would be worth ten thousand dollars. This man's prediction rested entirely on his faith in America's potential for growth. Indeed, Buffalo's population grew from 1500 in 1810 to over ten thousand in 1850. During my visit, somebody offered Brisbane fifteen thousand dollars for his plot of land, and he declined the offer.

Two hundred years hence, the land we now call America consisted of vast deserted spaces. Today, almost twenty-four million people call this land home. In the last twenty years alone, the population grew by ten million, and it is predicted that at least twenty-five million more people will settle in American within the next twenty-five years. In Europe our civilization stagnates and grows increasingly corrupt; instead in America, civilization is like a mighty river that flows and enriches all of its environs. America represents an ascending civilization, with lifeblood running through the fabric of society; it bursts with vigor, conquers nature, transforms deserts, innovates and thus embarks upon a great journey toward social progress, the evolution of which surpasses anything we have ever known in Europe.

If we leave these general considerations aside and return to our original topic, we can assert that the prodigious singularities that define American progress not only extend to Texas, but are poised to play an even more significant role in its growth. Never has a prediction been based on more solid grounds. One simply needs to reflect upon the wealth of assets on which this state will build its future in order to realize what a solid foundation this stage provides. The prodigality of Texas' natural surroundings presents settlers with ideal conditions to work, transform and prosper.

Who then makes up this army of settlers briskly conquering Texas? These people are poor, often destitute, scattered, uneducated and lacking capital, tools, skills, and contacts. When they arrive, they often establish isolated homesteads with neighbors living five, ten, fifteen and sometimes even twenty miles from each other. They remain divided, with no shared areas and no division of labor that is common in more densely populated areas. Each settler is self-sustaining and self-reliant. Almost every settler in North Texas grinds his own corn and grain in order to produce a substance akin to bread, consumed with every meal. Each settler must do everything himself in order to survive. He must fell his own timber; build rudimentary furniture; construct tools; and even fashion his own saddle. He is capable of riding forty to fifty miles to a farrier or to restore a plough.

Yet don't think for a moment that this depravation results in an excess of individual labor—not at all! Indeed, the Texas pioneer is not overburdened with work. Thanks to the lavishness of the Texas environment, he can rest during part of the year while reaping the bounty of his surroundings, from the livestock and the available commodities to the appreciation of his land, as he awaits Civilization, with its culture and comforts, to catch up with him. The lack of organized trade renders its convenience elusive and the process is stymied by intermediaries. If truth be told, trade in America is not driven by the principal that manifold small trades produce large profits; instead, the practice that is preached is that large trades produce great fortunes.

VIII

The way in which the settlers organized their communities in the areas of Texas relevant to our cause is entirely opposed to the order defined in our Process of Series. These pioneers live in a state of unsociability unbeknownst even to wild animals, the latter at least live in packs or in herds. It is difficult to summon a more incongruous approach to the establishment of a settlement than the fractional, inadequate social framework of these pioneers. Notwithstanding their dedication to a state of absolute social isolation and their commitment to the principal of allotment, these pioneers succeed in creating a society of great wealth.

Ah! Our confusion only added to our astonishment at the settlers' success! How could this remoteness, and this lack of social structure, industry and materials enable this immense wave of prosperity to develop along the coast and garner strength as it barrels north, unconstrained? As we contemplated the munificent nature that surrounded us and appraised the opportunities that it afforded those who recognized its facile and cooperative disposition, we could not help but shudder with excitement, anticipation, and anxiety. We were as impatient to apply our collective, superior intellect to begin our conquest of these wild lands as we were anxious that we would not be capable to suitably impart the spellbinding allure of this place that prodigiously captivated our minds and our souls. I thought to myself, "Surely they will believe me! They will not doubt what I have seen!" I wondered if my words alone could sufficiently convey the magnificence that we experienced; would they be enough to awaken your desire to rise and vanquish this new world, or would you deem the distance insurmountable and lapse into the torpor that infects our European brothers? Would my effort to put into words the reality that we witnessed triumph and convince you that we had found, beyond any doubt, the Promised Land, the place where we would find elation and fulfillment? These were the questions that pre-occupied my mind and unsettled my soul.

IX

Although I was apprehensive that I might not be able to fully convey the current social and environmental conditions in Texas, I am now certain that, upon reading my report, you will clearly recognize that the wholly auspicious surroundings I describe will convince you that our work there will generate great prosperity.

Indeed, in this nascent society, settlers must organize and adapt all the structural and social components commonly implemented in developed countries, from industry and trade to education and science. So many common aspects of society are entirely absent, mainly due to the area's incessant growth and the formidable accessibility to opportunities that create material wealth. A lone settler certainly makes do without certain elements; however, a settlement equipped with even the most ordinary components could coax an even greater degree of prosperity from the land's ample natural elements.

Brisbane and I encountered one such instance when we traveled across the Texas prairie and were accompanied by a constant procession of carts that transported enormous bales of cotton. We wondered if it wouldn't benefit farmers to establish hydraulic presses in determined locations along the river, similar to those used by British soldiers to transport fodder in Spain during the 1803 war. When we reached Galveston, Texas' largest port, we learned that there was a cotton press in the city, and that its three owners each earned three hundred dollars per day. Even if this amount seems exaggerated, it remains undisputable that an enormous quantity of product must be delivered to the mill in order to create such profits.

Based on what you now know about Texas weather, and in particular the prevalence of atmospheric currents throughout the State, you will understand why I believe that there is no other place on earth more auspicious for the use of windmills—not even Holland! Well, it will surprise you to learn that there is not one single windmill in all of Texas! Men forge wood planks with axes and families mill their grain with handheld grinders. In larger settlements, we sometimes encountered ox or mule carousels. If one were to manufacture and install windmills throughout the state, one could attain rapid and significant returns.

I will stop myself from enumerating more examples. I will simply add that those of us who seek to develop enterprises that makes use of simple tools such as awls, sewing machines, and other tools that meet the needs of the local population, stand to profit greatly from these sorts of endeavors. A small community of settlers who collaborate to manufacture goods and facilitate the transport of their products will benefit not only themselves, but also their neighbors, and in so doing, will yield even further profits.

X

Understand that poverty in Texas is not the same resigned and stagnant poverty that has been a habitual state for certain populations in Europe for centuries. Quite the contrary: In Texas poverty is merely a transitory state, a beginning or a departure point. Affluence and abundance hurtle alongside it and sweep up those in its path. Besides the natural advantages present in Texas, this prevailing ethos captured my attention as it further supports the suitability of Texas as the location to build our community.

Prosperity is generated so quickly and so profusely throughout this society that virtually every nucleus becomes its own center for the production of wealth, which in turn radiates outwards toward other individuals. This interchange produces a constant and powerful reciprocity that in turn generates more prosperity. To my knowledge, presently, there is no other place on earth where combined circumstances—industriousness, creativity, progress—create a more ideal stage for assured and profuse profit. Nowhere is the transition from poverty to wealth more widespread and certain, particularly since Texas remains an essentially agricultural society.

These auspicious circumstances will undeniably remain prevalent in the near future; however, I believe it is in our best interest not to waste any time in order to take advantage of the incongruously favorable extant climate. "Why?" you might ask; because Texas' reputation is rapidly spreading, especially among those who live in the North. Their gaze is turning south and they will soon begin to migrate as the railroad expands. Those who establish themselves in Texas before this influx stand to profit greatly from the business opportunities generated by these new arrivals.

It is worth noting that the swift forward momentum in America accelerates progress and spurs the dynamic development of affluence throughout the United Sates; this condition remains inconceivable to many Europeans who endure their ubiquitous quagmire. Everywhere in America new life springs forward with extraordinary abundance and energy. We need to grasp these surges of vitality as we consider the establishment of our settlement.

To better elucidate these great advantages, I decided to include the details from a document that I read during my transatlantic journey back to Europe. The information, recently published in Philadelphia, confirms my previous observations and also adds relevant details to this report. Below you will find my translation of the document in question.

XI

Texas. Soil composition, etc . . .

The region rests on a vast, sloping plain, interlaced with waterways, that gradually descends from the western peaks toward the southeastern regions, where it bleeds into the grasslands that border the coastline.

One distinguishes three distinct zones. The first, a low-lying region that encompasses the plains that begin at the gulf and extends along a band that measures fifty to one hundred miles in width. Unlike the swampy coastal areas common to its neighboring Southern states, this Texas region is exceedingly fertile due to its alluvial soil. Magnificent woodlands track the banks of its rivers where grasslands flourish. The next region encompasses an extensive area of undulating prairies, intersected by forests, and covered with robust vegetation that grows from a siliceous soil rich in limestone, and excellent for farming. The third region, known as the Mexican Alps, consists of fertile plateaus and extraordinarily fruitful valleys, capable of producing enough to recompense a farmer one hundred-fold. Without a doubt, Texas' expansive lands offer some of the most auspicious agricultural conditions anywhere on earth.

Varieties of trees abound throughout the state; the species include oak, especially live oak, hickory, elm, walnut, sycamore, acacia, and cypress. The mountain regions produce beautiful cedars and various pine trees, and a great variety of fruit trees and other garden vegetables grow easily and abundantly: peaches, melons, grapes, and other fruit. In the southern part of the state, one finds a profusion of tropical fruits such as oranges, figs, lemons, and olives.

Main crops include cotton, corn, wheat, barley, and other grains; sugar cane; potatoes; rice; tobacco; indigo; vanilla; and even sassafras. The prairies are home to large herds of cattle and flocks of sheep, and also large numbers of mules and pigs, all of whom feed indiscriminately on the endless reserve of grasses. Enormous herds of buffalo and wild horses also roam these lands that teem with all types of game as well as deer, and even bears. No state in the Union remotely equals the richness of the Texas pastureland.

Indians

Hordes of Indians continue to pervade the territory. These natives continue to conduct destructive and often times bloody forays and depredations. Local settlers incessantly endeavor to establish peaceful and friendly relationships with the marauders; however, until the area's population increases, this desired outcome will most likely not be met. In 1850, the population of Texas consisted of the following groups:

Whites: 154,000
Free Blacks: 551
Slaves: 58,161
Total: 212,552

Climate

Travelers and setters alike agree that Texas enjoys a delightful, healthy climate throughout the state, with few exceptions.

As in California, winters, also referred to as the rainy season, begin in December and end in March. The remainder of the year—spring, summer, and fall—consists of the dry season. Winter is mostly mild; snow is infrequent and falls mostly on the western summits. The summer heat can be intense, but it is tempered by the customary daily breezes that last from sunrise to mid-afternoon. Throughout the year, the nocturnal air remains refreshing. From April to September, the temperature fluctuates between 65 and 100 degrees Fahrenheit, with a midday average of 85 degrees. During the summer, fevers spread throughout the low-lying regions along the gulf, however, their presence never reaches epidemic proportions.

XII

To really appreciate this report, you must understand how people previously viewed the State of Texas. Its location at the southern extremity of the Union, its low-lying beaches along the gulf and the lore surrounding its inhabitants all contributed to its questionable—yet entirely false—reputation. Texas was thought to be one of the most lawless, dangerous areas of the Union: a haven for robbers and bandits of all stripes as well as fierce indigenous populations, secessionists, and adventurers as wild as the local Caddo and Comanche Indians. Countless people warned us about Texas before our departure and their descriptions painted a less than appealing image.

The document I shared with you demonstrates to what extent it is possible to see the errors of one's way. Its author presents Texas as we saw it, except that his description of the dry and rainy seasons is false in that rains occur intermittently throughout the year, a fact confirmed by many settlers in Texas. As to the wild nature of the inhabitants, nothing could be farther from the truth!

Intermittent forts dot the frontier. These structures consist of simple wooden shacks, with garrisons of barely fifty to sixty men. We thought to ourselves that these soldiers must hardly fear the Indians as they only use wooden gates as barriers to protect themselves.

The evening we arrived in the town of Preston, we

settled at an inn started by a husband and wife who had traveled there eight years hence from Virginia. The wife told us that when they first arrived in the area, there were very few whites, and every night, she fully expected to be murdered. When her husband traveled, she would sit by the door all night, awake and holding a large stick, ready to defend herself and her property. This tiny woman bore more semblance to a doll than to an athlete; we concluded that the supposed wild hordes that lived in Texas must not have been so fearsome after all.

The falsehoods and distorted tales about the swashbuckling life on the Texas frontier have been perpetuated by distance and hearsay. When told by a braggart, a story about two men in pursuit of a horse robber becomes a tale about expeditions and campaigns against gangs of thieves and wild Indians. As we traveled though Texas, we spoke to hundreds of settlers, and witnessed life on the frontier firsthand; we soon recognized that the anecdotes we had heard were illusory and that Texas was safer than the streets of New York, London, or Paris. Of course, one cannot say that the white men who inhabit Texas are all model citizens; however, it is safe to say that the majority are upstanding people, especially the farmers. In fact, it is so easy to earn a proper living in Texas that beggars have no reason to live there and crimes are limited to, for the most part, petty theft. People go to Texas first and foremost to produce, trade and farm; on the whole, Texas is among the safest regions I have ever encountered.

Albeit Texas did not enjoy a stellar reputation in the past, I can assure you that a bright and favorable light begins to shine on the land within its borders and it beckons capital, industry, and speculators from the North. I will add a personal anecdote to corroborate this observation. When we returned to Galveston from Austin, we encountered a group of established businessmen from New York who anticipated investing substantially in real estate. Tracks are already being laid to extend the transcontinental railroad into the Trinity River valley along the Red River. At the rate railroads are being stretched throughout the United States, one thing is certain: if the Union-Pacific railroad does not come directly through this area, one of its most important branches will certainly traverse North Texas.[2]

At this point, you must think that I have exhausted all the comments that relate to the vitality and prospects that combine to make Texas an ideal destination for our community. No, my friends! I have so many more accolades to report! The next topic I will discuss is the cost of Texas land.

---

2. As I edited this chapter, I received an updated map of the Texas rail lines from Brisbane. I will discuss this further at the end of my report.

XIII

You must think: "Since it is a given that land in Texas is more fertile than in other States, its cost must be superior." Well friends, you stand corrected! Land in the other States costs one-and-a-quarter dollars per acre, whereas in Texas one can still purchase an acre of land for twenty cents an acre, the lowest cost of land per acre in all of the United States! Note that the land of which I speak is not limited to certain types of parcels. This is the price of any unclaimed land. Allow me to explain.

In the United States, all unclaimed lands belong to the Union, and it is all sold for the standard price of one-and-a-quarter dollars per acre. Texas, however, was an independent country before it joined the Union, and it retained ownership of its land when it became a state. Previous to this, during its war of independence from Mexico, in order to attract men to fight the Mexicans, Texas compensated these volunteers with land that was awarded in the form of bonds called headrights, which allowed the holder to choose his apportioned acreage from any available land in the state. These volunteers, most of whom were foreign adventurers, hastened to take advantage of their headrights, and the excessive availability of free land led to the devaluation of its actual worth.

Up until five years ago, land that was obtained with headrights was valued at five cents an acre. Its value has increased

100 percent; during our time in Texas, land was selling between eighteen and twenty-two cents an acre, the equivalent of one franc. I remind you about my earlier observations regarding this phase of rapid growth currently underway in Texas, and the need of our community to make a prompt decision so we can benefit from this ascendant phase. This is not all: in order to encourage settlements, all immigrants can purchase lots of five hundred and twenty acres of land, and with this, they receive a remuneration of twenty dollars. The cost of land de facto becomes fifty cents an acre.

In summary, five years ago, because of headrights, the price of land was twenty-five cents per acre, sixty cents per hectare. Today, the value increased to one franc per acre and two-point-five francs per hectare. A square league of sixteen hundred hectares valued at one thousand francs five years ago (because of headrights), is now worth four thousand francs. Due to its unique history, its immense expanse and the origins of its settlers, the cost of Texas land, the superiority of which is unchallenged, remains below the cost of acreage in other states.

XIV

You are now familiar with the natural elements as well as the social and economic circumstances that constitute the current state of affairs in Texas. I attempted to describe the totality of facts that contribute to the inalienable advantages of this state, as well as the unique historical circumstances that converged to create such a vigorous and emergent economy. Many young American states present similar sensations; however, in Texas, these circumstances become amplified. In part, Texas remained untouched because its richness had been hereto now unrecognized; fear also kept many potential setters at bay.

Alas, people in America are not the only ones to recognize Texas' potential; this reality has begun to emerge in Europe as well, as was recently proven by an excerpt from the *Annals of Commerce* that appeared in the *Monitor's* October 27 edition. The article invokes France's missed commercial opportunities as well as the current and future business prospects in Texas. Below are relevant passages from the *Monitor* article entitled *United States: Reports about Texas.*

"In 1852, it was reported that business in Galveston flourished at a rapid pace, along with the general prosperity of the entire State of Texas. Harvests, in particular those of cotton and sugar, doubled. Direct trade relations were established with Europeans, principally with Germany."

"Many immigrants arrived directly from Germany,

through the port of New Orleans. A great number of Americans came by land from the Eastern slave states where land continues to be depleted."

"It is regrettable that French commerce, deeply in need of new outlets, has not made any serious effort to exploit this new market, currently monopolized by the Germans. Without a doubt, this is to become the biggest center for sugar and cotton production in the United States."

"The climate of this new State is salubrious except for the marshy areas along the coast that are prone to incite dreaded fevers."

"Land is inexpensive: prices stretch from fifty cents to ten francs per acre[3] (*). Proximity to roads, rivers, towns and cities determines the value."

"Indians are not to be feared, except for those in the Western part of the State, along the Rio Grande. Yellow fever is mostly unknown in Texas, except in densely populated areas, at least one hundred miles from the sea. Here, the land elevates into undulating plains intersected by woods."

I outlined the components that contribute to the prosperity of this land; I described my disposition; I reported on all elements as I encountered them; I portrayed the natural assets and recounted all relevant historical circumstances. I have accomplished my mission. I will now allow you time to meditate on the elements of this extraordinary

---

3. The land selling for ten francs an acre is privately owned land, therefore this number is insignificant.

country, and I invite you to estimate the value of each of these factors and to calculate their potential return.

Understand that by reading my report you will know more about Texas than the vast majority of Americans, including most of those who inhabit Texas itself, who remain for the most part uncultured and uneducated, although they instinctually grasp the value of their new surroundings. To my knowledge, my report represents the first true account of Texas: a land blessed with a truly extraordinary amalgamation of conditions, that separately would already provide great value, where one can achieve great outcomes with relatively minimal resources.

I affirm my report on this date, November 1855, and I ask that it be noted. I realize that many years will pass before my pronouncements can be verified, therefore I ask that they be documented today, among ourselves.

PART THREE

PREPARATIONS

I

Now that you have read all there is to know about Texas, you may wonder what else I could possibly discuss. Well, my friends, in these next few pages you will find my further recommendations.

To begin with, I appeal to the Associative School to awake from its dormancy and to resuscitate its ideals. I appeal to all of us who are likeminded in thought and in spirit to unite and undertake a momentous project: the establishment of a society conscious of its means and of its goals whose members will adopt and apply the most advanced methods and ideas known to man in order to establish a space where freedom, enlightenment, and prosperity flourish, unrestrained.

I appeal to all my brothers to immediately emancipate the social Truth for which we are responsible by embracing this opportunity instead of perishing under the theoretical improbabilities and the torpors present in Europe, where hope has become listless and illusive to the point of unrighteousness. I appeal to each of you to unencumber yourselves and assertively resolve to overcome the moral somnolence, the acquiescence and the self-interest that suffocate social-ism in Europe today, in order to hail a new home where you can fulfill the ideas and ideals to which you have been so faithful. Although we might be separated by distance, we are united in spirit, and together we can resurrect the soul of our collective consciousness and resolve to create a Phalanx Community where we will endeavor to immediately bring forth our glorious plan.

Friends, I assure you, the Promised Land is a reality. I did not believe it, I did not seek it, but I was shown the way: we beheld the land and wandered through it during forty days, as I described. Redemption stirred within us! Believe in the Land of Fruition; this Promised Land is yours! With strong resolve and a collective act of faith, we will conquer it!

The bluntness of these words should not diminish the solemnity of my message: I unveiled the path forward, the path of salvation. Let us unite with determined courage and usher in new era! The Associative School encompasses more assets than this work demands. Let us unite and con-verge them; by so doing, the foundation can be set.

II

If my message reassures you; if it rouses you from slumber; if it ignites desire in your souls; if the mere thought of it incites the quiver of love, hope and faith, then you are baptized in our cause and you are ready to devote your heart and soul to our mission. Our noble and pious cause, conceived from the convergence of wills, is born. Our activity and our developing ideas will progressively nourish its fledgling soul.

I should now like to outline the nature and the progression of our actions. I will summarize the material needs as well as the logistics we must undertake, both as individuals and as a group, in order to execute this great work.

You will immediately discover the contrast between the rationale we will use to accomplish our mission in the new world and the one we would use if we remained in our current environment. More precisely, the old paradigm began with an isolated scientific trial limited to a restricted number of participants that narrowly followed the formula of the Process of Series. Whereas in our new milieu, from the very beginning, our living conditions will include elements apt to position us for success. In our European experiments, in was a matter of dedicating capital to a predetermined procedure to anticipate the results. I remind you all that I obstinately opposed the attribution of predetermined funds for a Process of Series experiment in Europe. I insisted on the following three points, hundreds of times:

The first Process of Series experiment would be an expensive undertaking;

The first Process of Series experiment would not improve the fate of those who participate in its creation and development in the near future;

The first Process of Series experiment would certainly necessitate an extended course that might require participants to commit considerable amounts of personal capital, which would not have been a fair expectation.

The Associative School generally accepted the fact that it would pursue its objectives for its own interest, for its own sovereign cause, and for the triumph of universal good for humanity. It was founded on its selfless devotion to its cause. Today, after having proved its worth, commitment no longer demands sacrifice; rather, the School expects its followers to vigorously seize the paths to achievement afforded to them in order to bring to fruition the cause with which they were entrusted.

I'm certain that you now grasp how the old methods have changed in favor of new, significantly improved ones, and you must no doubt anticipate the great actions that lie ahead, as you become familiar with the information I share in this report. For us, and here I speak both for Brisbane and myself, once we grasped the possibilities that extended before us, all previous discussions ceased. The breadth of the foundation on which we could establish our new community presented so many opportunities that we took this to be the nexus of our proposition. Let us now focus our attention on ascertaining this foundation.

III

When colonization takes hold of a new territory, the development of the colony depends on the concurrent pursuit of actions that individuals undertake at their own risk. This is certainly the case in America as a whole, especially in the new States and the Confederate Territories.[4]

Nevertheless, the situation alters when it comes to the conquest of territories and the establishment of bases of operation, a process that remains thus far unresolved. The common instruments of civilized society have often proved to be inadequate, either because the initiatives centered around the principle of individual actions or because they resorted to one of collectivity.

The principle of individual actions is too weak to succeed, and the principle of collectivity, thus far incarnate in the rudimentary and crude form of the community, has never been capable of prospering unless instituted on the basis of fervent religious faith. In general, the trade companies based and operated in Europe that engage with new

---

4. There are currently thirty-three states in the United States; in addition, there is the District of Columbia, administered directly by Congress whose seat is located within the district. Six additional territories are destined to become states once their population increases; currently they are administered by the United States government. Further, the Indian Territories remain independently governed by Indian tribes.

territories initially failed; at the very least, they experienced very difficult beginnings.

In Texas, whether we choose to establish ourselves in the north or the northwest, we will not face the hazards associated with the conquest of a completely new territory as many surrounding areas have already been settled; yet we will not find ourselves in the midst of an already proven colony. Since we should not seek to mimic their spread-out parceling, we will need resolve how we plan to execute and develop our venture prior to our departure. We will find a clear path forward if we apply the Process of Series to determine the value of each step in our development with the series of successive approximations. This is where we will begin.

IV

General and principal notion

The primary and fundamental design for our settlement in Texas centers around the establishment of a new form of society, innovative both in structure and in its very nature, which is determined by the purpose and the progression of its creation. We will build our foundation on several elements in order to achieve our goal of Social Harmony: the rapid development of material prosperity; the fulfillment of social progress; the adherence to science, freedom, truth, solidarity, and distributive justice; and the combination and converging of spontaneous individual actions. We will apply practical experimental procedures as we advance toward a society where its members experience the refinement of human social interactions.

Now that we established this premise, we will define the initial element in the Process of Series, in other words, we will estimate its initial practical value, or the conditions necessary for its implementation.

V

First appraisal

We will establish and develop our Associative Community according to the progressive creation of the structure and mechanisms needed to ensure the sequential and anticipated phases of its existence.

The initial mechanism we will need to establish is a Settlement Agency that will be untrusted with two primary functions:

1/ acquire lands where the first nuclei of our society will live,

2/ make all the necessary arrangements to prepare this land for the arrival of the first groups of settlers.

The subsequent phase consists of the arrival of the settlers themselves who will be free to live according to their own beliefs.

In order to ensure the creation of material prosperity needed to achieve the society's ultimate ambition of absolute freedom and peace, the Settlement Agency will need to purchase a significant expanse of land. Since there are already significant settlements in southern Texas, and both the climate and natural conditions in north and northwestern Texas are superior to those in other parts of the State, it seems obvious that we will focus on purchasing land in these latter regions.

Once this purchasing phase is complete, the Settlement Agency will proceed to make the necessary arrangements to prepare for the arrival of the first wave of settlers. These members will be chosen based on their aptitude to fulfill actual tasks as well as their dedication to our founding design; these stipulations will all be outlined in a contract composed by these men and representatives of the Settlement Agency. The settlers will remain entirely autonomous and fully free to direct their own affairs and pursue their own interests.

Once this first settlement takes root, it will naturally prepare the groundwork for new arrivals, while the Settlement Agency continues to organize the succeeding contingents, thus allowing for a continuous flow of arrivals.

Herein lies the first phase of our development; in other words, this is the assessment of the first mechanism needed for the implementation of our mission. Although this is but an outline, it contains the essential and fundamental characteristics of our plan. A more detailed plan will be based on a precise substantiated analysis.

VI

Second appraisal

Characteristics of the foundation - Even though this initiative retains the characteristics of a phalansterian society, you will remark that its realization does not strictly adhere to the particular plan of a phalanx; rather, the initiative is more wide-ranging, and it also permits experimentation with various practical norms common to other progressive doctrines that uphold the notions of personal risks and responsibility. This proposal does not invite phalansterians to go to Texas and establish the first society based on the Process of Series and to build a phalanx. To suggest this course of action would be highly imprudent as it would most certainly lead to failure.

Instead, for this Texas settlement, we tender to our members the foundation of a society bound and united by its faith in progressive ideals, established in surroundings that are inherently hospitable and favorable to the rapid development of prosperity, which in turn will allow its members the means to live according to these ideals. Although the goal of the Associative Community would remain the realization of its original social process, they should restrain their inclination to immediately apply the rules of the associative system in order to establish the settlement; as stated, this can nevertheless remain the ultimate objective. I will subsequently include guidance related to a new systematic design.

Logic demands that the settlement process make use of the means most readily available at the point of settlement. This requires distancing oneself from the natural inclination toward the use of preconceived notions and systems, as their strict application may hinder the settlement process. The objectives of each progressive doctrine can subsequently be recalled and the particular social process harnessed, as long as these are not enforced prematurely.

The essential nature of this proposal is easy to grasp: it is a matter of creating a vast field of social activity in an area where the first order of business is communal prosperity, not the innovation of social experiments. Foresight and solidarity in preparations, including the choice of lands rich in natural resources, combined with freedom of individual initiatives as well as the implementation of established procedures, provide the circumstances that nurture humankind's progressive thought, which has been rebuffed, stifled, and vilified in the name of socialism by Europe's old guard.

This notion encompasses more than the associative principles of collective organization; it conforms to our doctrine's advanced principles that direct us to zealously seek the unconditional advancement of humanity. Indeed, this represents the formal application of the theory of scientific and affirmative conditions of social progress that our School notably was the first to introduce and will now have the opportunity to authenticate. We will put in place the practical conditions to fulfil our theories on the institution of social progress, and we invite others who seek to implement likeminded doctrines to join us in our quest to aid humanity.

I realize that this concept is grand and requires unwavering faith in our doctrines and in our ability to maintain social harmony as well as unconditional love for the welfare of humankind. Nevertheless, this noble and sweeping experiment is indisputably the most certain path to accomplish our purpose.

Preservation of the social objective - The success of our fundamental objective clearly rests on the sustenance of the beliefs and desires that prompted our mission. We must equip those who dedicate their minds and spirits to the actualization of this idea with all necessary means to succeed. A doctrine becomes an institution thanks to the vigor of the minds it enlists; a belief incarnates its tangible form thanks to the deliberate and creative actions of those who sustain it.

When you allow an idea free rein to develop; when you provide it with the means to sustain itself; when you allocate the indispensable sustenance to shape a solid and functioning structure, you nurture a soul who will in turn give birth to the body to which it aspires.

Acquisition of land - Next, I will share a few thoughts regarding the Settlement Agency's initial orders of business as well as the extent of primary land acquisition.

The reasons to purchase considerable tracks of land were explicitly discussed earlier in this report. It would be clearly senseless not to invest in the land where we intend to develop a venture designed to welcome increasing population and capital. We must also purchase large tracks of land in order to protect ourselves from foreign speculators.

The lack of a significant investment would represent a missed opportunity; we would in fact act against our own growth since foreign speculators would quickly seize the chance to purchase lands adjacent to our developed acreage. We run the risk of becoming encircled by others while we continue to develop our community in an increasingly constricted area.

Given the reasonable cost of land and the magnitude of our intended project, we must prepare to acquire a significant expanse of land while its cost remains affordable. In fact, what risk does the purchase of land actually represent? Even if we do not endeavor to develop the land, its value would continue to rise as the population grows. The value of headrights alone has quadrupled in the past five years. These are clear indicators that the acquisition of properly selected land in Texas is a sound investment. Let me conclude that, based in this compelling evidence, we will proceed accordingly.

Preparation of the acreage - This topic is of upmost importance. Indeed, many undertakings failed because those who organized these initiatives, either because of ignorance or because of misplaced hope and enthusiasm, did not properly ready their land prior to the arrival of the first waves of settlers. It is almost certain that we will fail if we send a group of settlers, particularly European settlers, to virgin lands without assuring prior preparation. It is true that in Texas our settlers would be capable of finding individual success; however, this would not lead us to our objective of a collective society.

In the annals of modern settlements, you will find ample evidence that demonstrates the absurdity of transplanting people from an organized society to a foreign location where they encounter no social structure, and where the establishment of a new society relies wholly on improvisation. I shall therefore not waste my time on the elaboration of these facts and I will assume that we all forthwith accept the need for prior preparation.

I therefore recommend that we agree on a tenet whereby, upon their arrival, the setters must encounter living conditions equal to those they left behind, in addition to certain structures, to facilitate rapid growth. This premise must become the keystone of our endeavor. We must base our actions on certitudes in order to plan our strategy so as to avoid extending ourselves beyond our capabilities. Let us not become transfixed by the golden hue of illusions.

VII

Institution of the founding values

It is evident that nature dictates the terms of development, and each of these terms will be rated according to its relevance to our initial group of setters. Indeed, this first group, whose composition is yet undetermined, will become the embryo of our new society as these settlers will secure the basic elements on which our society will develop and prosper. First, they will determine their adaptability and their capacity for expansion; next they will create transportation networks to facilitate trade and the safe movement of new settlers. These routes must interconnect with navigable waterways and other main travel lanes in order to henceforward establish a safe and expedient route for other settlers.

In order to encourage settlers to join our cause, we must do everything in our power to facilitate their voyage. Once they arrive by ship to the ports closest to our settlement, or eventually to the closest rail station, they will be greeted by stagecoaches owned and operated by our community. After their long voyage, the settlers and their belongings will be transported directly to their destination. The Settlement Agency will actually coordinate their entire passage, from Paris or any other European port, to their arrival in New

York or New Orleans. Once we establish the routes, the process will be simple and we can regularize the flow of arrivals.

Let us consider the parameters of our new settlement: the span of the land; the climate; the ease with which one can erect new buildings (we will subsequently examine this topic in depth). You will clearly recognize that our community will promptly be able to welcome new arrivals who will be immediately lodged and employed in a multiplicity of enterprises: agriculture, industry, and all manners of workshops. These lodgings would of course be temporary and the new settlers can build homes that better suit the needs of their individual families.

My comments on this topic suffice as I wish to remain faithful to the deductive method that I vigorously respected thus far. Given the details I provided and your keen understanding of our methodology, I am certain that you fully grasp the nature of the mission that awaits us; our undertaking represents the creation of a living being. This living being is a society, and the social conditions that result from its founding become in and of themselves living organisms. We have conceived a social embryo that conforms to the known development process of a physiological embryo.

Through this act of conception, we give birth to this societal organism that will develop its own nature and spirit. We will provide an embryonic brain, the Settlement Agency; we will recognize the need to provide an environment for its incubation; and finally, we will equip it with the elements it needs to sustain itself and grow, and eventually to propagate.

VIII

I do not wish to lose myself in too many details regarding the laws of embryonic development; I merely wish to draw your attention to the empirical significance of this comparison. You will observe that although the process of natural development follows a determined path, its outcomes are varied. In the case of our social embryo, we can state that it differs from an organic embryo just as an emerging embryo differs from a developed one. The physical embryo begins its external functions and activities after its birth, whereas the social embryo, such as the one we will create, will be conceived as a fully operational and interactive entity whose integral monads are not nascent beings; they are able, functioning elements.

The attempt to apply of the laws of embryonic development to the progressive creation of our social being might be viewed as a sophomoric rationalization; however, I ask you to bear with me as I elaborate this comparison to illustrate our endeavor. The general law that governs the development of life itself, without a doubt, extends to this new creation, the social being; however, this being will foster a new sequence of development whereby it will emerge as a fully developed embryo from the moment of its initial conception. Any disciple of our Associative School, who is well versed in the philosophy of science, will fully grasp the implications of this observation, on which I refrain to elaborate for fear that I would fill another volume with my comments. I will add that the knowledge of the laws of nature that pertain to human development represents the foremost characteristic of a superior pragmatic mind.

Rest assured that we will succeed thanks to our knowledge of these laws, whereas others, who disallow their significance, risk total failure. I defy those who have alleged experience with matters of settlements, along with available assets to invest (I do not begrudge them this advantage), to establish anything other than a fragmented settlement where land is simply parceled out among the incomers who disdain one essential element: a social structure. In order to succeed, settlers must be inherently united by a common plan and a common faith, or better still, by a common faith coupled with the understanding of the laws of nature that pertain to natural development. Without these elements, their efforts become unsustainable and their undertaking collapses. Certain individuals might prosper while harsh natural conditions cripple many other lives; the communal enterprise that never properly took root completely dissolves.

IX

We outlined the general conditions for our undertaking, and we drafted the embryonic process through which our social being transforms itself from intertwined primitive organisms to complex, structured ones that will bond to create a flawless, collective union. We have established our foundation and we can continue our analysis.

Given that we understand the initial impetus as well as the other general conditions existent at its inception, it becomes evident that the project's general development hinges primarily on one condition: the creation of a system that can guarantee proper alimentary sustenance.

Furthermore, we acknowledge that this system, capable of sustaining growth, will itself require an appropriate foundation. We can therefore pose two questions in order to guide its design:

First, what conditions does the embryonic state of this system require; and second, what is the nature and structure of this system.

I. Organization of the Preliminary Environment

In order to determine the structure of this environment, we must simply ask ourselves what function it shall fulfill, who will be responsible for its establishment and how will we implement these tasks.

X

PURPOSE

The purpose of this preliminary environment consists of welcoming and sheltering the first constituents called upon to found the community, and also provide them with a base from which this organism will derive. These constituents will be the first European and American settlers. Upon their arrival, it is essential that they encounter a facile and receptive environment that is sufficiently robust to nurture and sustain the seedlings of the emerging social being.

Now that we have established the principal to dictate the conditions prior to the arrival of the actual first settlers, we can outline the elements that the settlers must encounter upon their arrival:

A) Shelters that offer a certain degree of comfort and suitable to various individuals.

B) A system that can guarantee proper food supply which includes adequately stocked warehouses, planted fields, fruitful gardens, as well as herds of cattle, hogs, sheep, and all types of farm animals. In addition, we must provide the machinery and workshops needed to transform the raw material into consumable products: mills, ovens, kitchens along with the appropriate tools.

C) A practice to procure the raw materials needed to produce clothes, shoes, and all other types of apparel.

D) In addition to these three conditions indispensable to the material existence and comfort of the settlers, the initial environment must also feature prospective work in which the constituents can immediately engage, therefore these first incomers will be chosen on the basis of their ability to perform certain essential jobs: farmer, blacksmith, wheelwright, tailor and such other types of critical labor.

These four fundamental orders of business require the creation of commercial structures to ensure the proper flow and distribution of production, and also to administer the maintenance of existing equipment as well as the procurement of other indispensable tools.

XI

AGENTS AND IMPLEMENTATION

It is clear that the agents who will organize this base of operations must be experienced in the tasks required to ready this environment for the incomers. We will therefore call upon American pioneers to lead this incursion as they are well practiced in all matters pertaining to land preparation. Our capable and resolute associates in America await our signal. If these men are the generals, who might the soldiers be? Other local men who will be hired under analogous circumstances.

In America, Irish and German immigrants are contracted to perform all manners of manual labor from digging canals to laying train tracks. It is common knowledge that German workers are preferred over the Irish. Our experienced and competent American friends will therefore hire qualified laborers who will transform the wild prairie into arable fields and gardens, thin out and clear the forest, and erect the structures to welcome our settlers. They will assemble mechanical saws and a mill shipped from Pittsburgh or Cincinnati. Meanwhile, herds of cattle, hogs and sheep will graze on the surrounding land where they will grow and rapidly proliferate.

This practice is well established and with the right men to oversee the labor, it will evolve effortlessly.

During this phase, we should also consider a few of our European brothers, particularly nurserymen: one to tend to viticulture, one to tend to viniculture, and another to tend to horticulture. Subsequently we would also send one or two herdsmen, along with their dogs, from Lorraine, Hungary, or New Mexico, who are experienced at driving very large herds. The agricultural specialists will play an important role in the early success of the settlement.

What I have outlined thus far should not present any considerable obstacles, provided that we have the necessary capital and the right agents in America. Let us now broach the second subject.

II. Establishment of the first core of settlers

Although this topic is more complex, we will analyze the conditions, probe our beliefs, and determine the proper path to follow. As we begin to consider the issues that surround the establishment of a new settlement, distinct sequential phases emerge. The first issue that we must resolve can be explained as follows: by what means do we hypothesize about the assorted concrete conditions required to shape the initial phase of the settlement, once the preparation phase is complete? We will determine the conditions by considering the subsequent points:

1/ the function of the phase,

2/ the nature of its integral elements,

3/ the needs of those elements,

4/ the organizational process needed to carry out this phase.

XII

Development of the initial phase of the first voyage

Determination of the function of the phase

The first settlement will serve a double purpose: it will be responsible for its own sustainability and development, and it will immediately serve as a settlement agency to encourage expansion into the surrounding areas. The primary focus during this initial phase will center on the production of raw material and food needed to sustain the settlers so they can accomplish their objectives.

In accordance with the laws of embryonic development, the first phase of development emphasizes sustenance in order for the physical being to properly mature, before it can undertake basic interactions with others, and eventually engage in more sophisticated social exchanges. As such, our settlers will initially tend to their immediate material needs.

We can conclude that the natural and intrinsic function of the initial phase consists of the ability to consistently supply the base materials required for its growth. There is no need to revisit the matter.

XIII

Determination of the nature of the integral elements

To determine the nature of the integral elements, we can simply analyze the functions that they must fulfill during the initial phase. We can therefore deduce that these elements, the first settlers, must include large numbers of farmers and others who can tend to the production and transformation of raw materials, followed by workers skilled in all manners of essential trades and artistries.

Can we rely on this simple empirical formula to determine how to proceed? It almost seems too crude and straightforward. Yet I wonder how this simple principle was eschewed by so many whose attempted settlements failed so miserably. Why did they not observe these modest yet obvious preemptive rules?

Nothing is simpler or more transparent to understand than the truths that derive from within natural and scientific sequences. This qualifies as the first reason to follow this rigorous order as it outlines how to approach and resolve complex and evolving conditions. This thorough method is further compelling because it relies on common sense, instinct, and on irrefutable imperatives accepted by all, and to which we can agree to adhere for the common good.

So many times, the failure to recognize the relevance and value of this rigorous method predestined legitimate undertakings to become epic disasters. Remember if you will the French Republic's hastily organized 1818 emigration to Algeria; the 1812 phalansterian emigration to Brazil; and the communist expedition initiated in 1817 by M. Cabet intended to establish an Icarian colony in America. There are too many examples to name in these pages.

Many settlements owe their weak foundation to their neglect of these simple rules, which frequently led to the reliance on solely the integral elements for the preparation phase as well as the erroneous assessment to include only feeble numbers of farmers and other skilled workers. These were precisely the circumstances that caused the collapse of the phalansterian settlement of Brook Farm in America. I could name dozens of similar situations.

Let us therefore remain heedful of our reliable method and continue with this line of reasoning; this brings us to our third factor.

XIV

Determination of the needs of the integral elements

In view that these elements are men, we posit that their needs fall into three categories: material, nonphysical and intellectual. They are bound by their faith in their common cause.

M) The material needs will be amply provided by the men who arrived during the preparation phase and were chosen for their skills in performing necessary manual tasks. As a side note, we must ensure the continued physical health of the settlers with a structured exercise regimen. I recommend we provide them with ample opportunities to engage in equestrianism and swimming. Indeed, the settlers will discover the benefits of becoming practiced equestrians as the Texas prairie is hardly a place where one travels on foot.

N) Form the onset, we must plan to create occasions to satisfy the intellectual needs of the settlers. These activities should aim to elevate their mental capabilities and stimulate their aspirations as well as their interests. First, we must put in place appropriate language classes, both in French and English, and we must create a library as well as reading clubs. We must ensure that we readily recognize the intellectual ambitions of the first settlers, tasked primarily with manual labor, and encourage them to view the pursuit of cultural activities as a noble ambition.

P) Two types of nonphysical needs exist: those of the individual and those experienced collectively. Both can be satisfied through the pleasure of social relationships and through artistic pursuits; this requires the organization of certain infrastructures such as public meeting areas, a school, a public hall that can be purposed for concerts and dances, a café and other such spaces where people can gather, learn, socialize and pursue activities of leisure. This should include a preliminary draft for a theater as the need for collective cultural experiences is as pressing as the need for arable fields and vegetable gardens.

Most importantly, what these needs require before all else is freedom, not in an abstract sense, as in the right and ability to live as one desires, but rather in a tangible manifestation of the principle. To achieve this, we must put in place measures that apply to all aspects of the private and public lives of the individuals and families of our settlers. We will soon continue our discussion of this fundamental principle.

X) Requirements for Unitéisme[5]

The arrival of the integral elements in Texas marks the beginning of our quest for social harmony through our observance of Unitéisme, for we remain devoted to the development, the nurturing, and the protection of a collective society. Although the elements will primarily devote

5. In Fourier's Phalansterian Theory this refers to man's inherent need for collective living

themselves to manual labor, they also represent the first men who responded to the call to create this new society. If their initial impetus is the desire for superior well-being, they also carry their faith for the creation of a greater human society founded in human solidarity.

This objective might not be achieved immediately; nonetheless, these noble aspirations must find immediate means to express themselves in an organized and accessible fashion. Therefore, I propose the following structure in which to develop our aspirational collective society.

X. a) To nurture and advance our commitment to the ideals of our collective society, Sundays will be devoted to the common discussion and elucidation of our social objectives. We will engage in communal dialogues about Unitéisme, religion and other topics that interest our settlers.

X. b) We will collectively debate all proposed public projects that relate to matters such as site beautification and other functional communal needs, such as religious gatherings. The frequency and the length of these deliberations will depend on the complexities of the desired undertakings.

X. c) The creation of all institutions that coalesce our social solidarity will be voted by our settlers. They will in turn determine who among them will undertake all acts pertaining to the instatement and administration of these institutions: credit and insurance; funds to guarantee benefits in case of illness or accidents; retirement funds for the elderly, etc . . .

We could undoubtedly institute these structures through

the drafting of a constitution to be approved by the settlers prior to our departure. This represents the more expeditious process adopted by most settlement expeditions; however, this process does not adhere to the scientific method of reasoning that must always direct our decisions.

Furthermore, this practice is erroneous because it precludes the input of those who will be affected by the charter and it does not consider the ideas and interests of the concerned parties. It is essential that institutions originate through organic actions rather than through passive approval. If they are derived freely and spontaneously, they become intrinsically suitable and proprietary, which in turn instills in them a much firmer moral authority. In addition, such an undertaking affirms a settlement's autonomy and its fundamental right to freedom, which constitute the foundation of the collective society.

XV

Thanks to the adherence to our scientific method, we are able to ascertain the composition of the first group of settlers:

1/ The manual laborers such as the farmers and the skilled workers will constitute the keystone of the community, in accordance with articles A), B), and C) described above.

2/ Those elements called upon to fulfill individual and collective needs of the settlers, in accordance with articles M), N), P), X.a), X.b), X.c), and Y).

We have now outlined the formula that will allow us to put in place the elements of the first phase.

XVI

Determination of the organizational process needed to carry out this phase

For this next process, more than for any other, we must avoid any randomness. As we examine this situation, we promptly recognize that this process has two phases. First, we must determine its structure, and next, we must determine how to develop the structure.

Let us suppose that we were to decree this process to the settlers; they would therefore be subject to an imposed structure. According to this scenario, these settlers become the means through which the experience is realized. This is in fact the system that has been used thus far in all Process of Series social experiments. Yet our present objective is not to simply conduct an experiment; our objective is to create a self-sufficient structure that survives, grows, and prospers of its own volition.

Based on this deduction, we can infer that the best structure will be determined by observing the patterns of interactions among the first settlers. Our understanding of the structure of these exchanges will guide our elaboration of the organizational process. We will achieve the desired procedural structure by first carefully scrutinizing the settlers' unrestricted interactions and then creating a process based on those interactions.

XVII

Let us reflect on the growth of a living organism in nature. Once a seed is implanted in an apposite embryonic environment, its progressive growth merely requires the proper sustenance in order to become a fully developed being. Let us assess how this process applies to our own organism.

Our environment is prepared: the seed, represented by the Settlement Agency, is ready to collect the appropriate sustenance for the first evolution of our organism; in other words, the agency is ready to receive the properly vetted, like-minded settlers. Once these elements are engaged, what organizational structure will they need? We don't know, and we won't understand how to create it until they live and interact in their new environment. Our only certainty is that, thanks to our adherence to this method, we created the proper environment in which our first embryo is able to fulfill its responsibilities and its objectives.

XVIII

I would like to take a moment to address a point that I imagine many of you are questioning. In fact, I presume that many of you are thinking: "How can it be that our plan does not include the creation of a phalanstery!" This concern seems perfectly appropriate, since our Associative School's principal objective for the past twenty years has been the creation of an agricultural and industrial phalanstery. In order to appease your impatience and frustration, I would like to explain the intention of my seemingly illogical proposal.

My friends, our mission here is the grandest one we have ever devised, and we must not shy away from the declaration of this fact. It involves nothing short of the creation of a state based on the free and collective expression of our objectives, a representation of the catholicity, or universality, of our beliefs. Our Associative School, which many misrepresent as a sect, was destined to undertake this glorious initiative, thanks to its sovereign and comprehensive doctrine. Logic dictates that our mission, conceived from phalansterian ideas, should be planned and implemented by our phalansterian brothers. Since you constitute the integral elements of this initiative, and I am one of you, I cannot withhold any truths from you, nor can I spare you any details for the sake of gaining your expeditious approval. It is important that we all enter this agreement on equal standing and that we uniformly and enthusiastically embrace the undertaking.

Thus, let me return to my explanation as to why I did not suggest that we create a phalanstery. To do so would entirely disrupt the general premise of our plan; instead of founding a society open to the most progressive social ideals, our social framework would become limited and stifled by relying exclusively on this single phalansterian principle.

The phalansterian doctrine sought to find an ideal social structure for humanity, and its initial propagation contributed significantly to social transformations. These ideas inspired others to promote doctrines that championed progressive social ideas. Indeed, our Associative School, bolstered by its apparent popularity, encouraged these other doctrines, even though they often presented inclinations that diverged significantly from its own principles. We have always recognized the value of this privileged position; the implementation of these rival doctrines drove us to elevate our own dogmas. This standing also bears irrefutable witness to the fact that our School unconditionally promotes social progress for the benefit of all humanity.

With this in mind, is it not preferable for us to adapt phalansterian doctrine to our overall objectives rather than to hasten the full expression of the School's principal objective, the creation of a Phalanx Community, since this would in fact diminish our freedom to act upon the local prospects and needs that will present themselves to us, and are yet unknown?

XIX

If we reduce our immediate objective simply to the building of a phalanstery, would we reach our ultimate goal, the establishment of a Phalanx Community, more expeditiously? I don't believe this would be the case. First, in general, the shortest path is not always the most constructive. Second, there exist abundant practical reasons why this path would derail us from our goal and might indeed compromise our entire mission. For over twenty years we studied the creation of the harmonic series and its expression in the Phalanx Community, and we debunked all the delusions concerning the assumed simplicity of this operation. We recognized that this endeavor stipulated several conditions, specific elements, and its creation would involve many glitches and setbacks. Further, this undertaking would have to be sufficiently supplied and constantly fortified in order to properly overcome all unforeseen circumstances.

These matters occupied us ceaselessly. You are all cognizant of the conclusions we drew from our exhaustive analysis; no issue was more thoroughly examined by our School, since the issue of harmonic seriisme represents the keystone of our doctrine.

Let us recall the conditions necessary to conduct this experimentation. Now, let us imagine how difficult, indeed impossible, it would be for our first settlers to encounter them, even partially, upon their arrival in a foreign land.

Many have put forth the idea of conducting an experiment in a foreign country and have urged us to build our community in a country that offered a blank canvas. It remains sufficiently challenging to assemble the funds to conduct an experiment in a civilized country, let alone in an unknown, barren country where we would have to create and ensure everything ourselves.

We reasonably established that our task was difficult enough, and it would become all the more complex if we added undetermined adversities. We concluded that it would be unconscionable to overburden ourselves with the obstacles inherent with the settlement in a foreign land when planning to create the first society structured on the principles of harmonic seriisme.

Yet, are these explanations still valid today, even though they were perfectly coherent at the time? Even though circumstances may change, rational principles do not; I will not pretend to ascertain that something is true today if I demonstrated that it was false in the past. Even though we exerted a great deal of effort to bring to light all the difficulties associated with the creation of Phalanx Community and strained to dispel any illusions in regard to the simplicity of this task, these illusions are likely to reemerge. Nevertheless, my ability to oppose this occurrence is limited, and I can only continue to hold fast to what I know to be true. Today, I stand resolute in my determination to personally graft our future in a distant land, and I invite those who adhere to the *out of civilization* doctrine to join me, as long as you bear in mind these admonitions: beware of your illusions; forsake the thought that your dream will swiftly come to fruition; relinquish your most ardent aspirations; be wary of your desire to reach your objective prematurely.

In order to embark on this mission, it must be absolutely understood that we will avoid all actions that might complicate our social experimentation and settlement efforts, even though, as I previously explained, these efforts will be greatly facilitated by extremely favorable conditions. Understand that our primary concern is to ensure the success of our settlements, for this is in the best interest of our social experiment. Indeed, the most effective means to pursue our social experiment is to ascertain the process necessary to develop, nourish and reproduce our settlements. We cannot compromise the settlements by imposing a specific structure on which to base their development; this would cause their growth, indeed their very existence, to be subjugated by a construct around which all other elements would have to revolve.

XX

The first settlement will not be constrained by any pre-existing dogma or by any previously wrought disposition. Its organization will be determined by the integral elements, the first settlers, who will base its configuration on the conditions imposed by their new environment.

XXI

Now that we have agreed upon this principle, we must anticipate all the possible exigencies that might exist in the initial preparatory phase. Let it be noted that this outline remains approximate as the integral elements must remain free to make their own determinations, unencumbered by compulsory restraints. They must encounter a wholly flexible environment capable of accommodating their choices.

Fortunately, the nature of our project as well as the prevalent local conditions our integral elements will encounter provide this necessary flexible environment. Thanks to the climate, the expansiveness of the location, and the ostensible ease with which we will be able to construct essential structures, this concept of flexible environment evolves from a simple theory to straightforward certainty.

The hostile climates, the elevated construction costs, as well as the limited territorial conditions that we have faced thus far in our own surroundings, compelled us to create compact, closely spaced buildings. In our new settlement, we will learn to adapt our architecture to the local climate and other existing environmental circumstances. Based on our observations, we already know that we must plan and position our structures in a way that they benefit fully from the expansive setting and the climate—especially the prevailing breezes. We can easily envision a series of independent pavilions linked together by a series of verandas or open galleries. Far from sacrificing a harmonious design for our community, this plan could efficiently satisfy our domestic requirements.

XXII

We are all familiar with the societal model that centers on the individual as this is the model in which we currently live. We can easily imagine the cooperative model, represented either by the phalansterian or communist example. Now, imagine the myriad possibilities and progressive outcomes if both these models—individual and cooperative—harmonized, unrestricted, in the same arena. Imagine the innovative paradigms this free association would produce!

This innovative model that I describe is none other than the concept for the new society we will found together.

Since we have already discussed the characteristics of the integral elements, we can now proceed to the account of the desired framework that will support the development of our settlers' work life. Let us remember that these conditions must accommodate both the individual and cooperative societal models.

We can assume that first settlers will be motivated to pursue the cooperative model. Such is the model of the North American Phalanx (N.A. Ph.) that simply adopted the basic, strictly economic principles of our theory. We should closely examine the experiment of the N.A. Ph. and deduct which elements we can reproduce, and possibly improve, during our initial efforts. In fact, as the point of departure for our cooperative model, we could envision duplicating the structure of the N.A. Ph., albeit with a more robust population, who will benefit from superior environmental conditions. We would of course be free to modify and improve this structure as we see fit.

Other settlers who do not wish to engage in this type of cooperative life can choose to establish independent homes, away from the main community. This in fact will help us develop a network of communication and facilitate travel and transportation of goods. It is safe to assume that these settlers will soon foster relationships among themselves, and they will discover how to cooperate on various projects.

The possibilities are endless: We can conceive and create anything we desire in this vast and welcoming space. We can fashion all types of cooperative agreements, as long as they are all rooted in the principal of reciprocity; some of these conventions will concern those who live in an associative setting, others will pertain to individuals, and others still will exist between individuals and the Associative Community. For instance, a family who chooses to live independently might decide to work in one of the community workshops or in the community fields. Others who choose a self-sufficient subsistence might want to share particular convivial aspects of cooperative life. Still other settlers will partially engage in cooperative life whilst exerting activities that benefit their individual families alone.

It is important to note that individuals and families are not beholden to a specific model and they are free to navigate from one type of model to another. The most important rule is *freedom and mutual respect*. Herein lies the template for the societal networks of our community. Although it is impossible to predict every type of connection that will exist, this framework provides us with a preliminary understanding of the functioning of our society.

Even though a portion of our settlers will choose to establish individual dwellings that stand apart from the cooperative community, it is safe to assume that these families will soon participate in the solidarity of our society, given that they their arrival was influenced, at least in part, by the very nature of our great *Idea* and its promise of mutual assurances and networks of collective guarantees. Clearly, this system, developed in the field and based on the real needs of the inhabitants of our community, produces a superior outcome than any of the societal systems advanced by the various European socialist schools of thought.

XXIII

I could stop my report here; I have concluded my project. The premise and the founding principles were explained and understood, and the mechanics for the process were determined through rigorous analysis and deduction. Henceforth, additional details will provide no practical value to the aforementioned particulars.

Nonetheless, since my explanations have thus far concerned ideological insights and hypothetical proceedings, allow me to provide a detailed description to clarify the realization of our mission. Even though the answer is not forthcoming, I am compelled to address this imperative question: what is the scale of our venture? The scope can easily run the gamut from small to large; all depends on the initial number of participants. If these are abundant, which I keenly desire, our undertaking will evolve at lightning speed and our success will be imminent. If the initial numbers are weak, our undertaking and its success will no doubt demand more time and effort; however, in either case, we will reach our objective.

In light of this uncertainty, let us therefore remind ourselves that the driving force remains our unwavering resolve to form a society, large or small, bound by laws derived from our beliefs.

XXIV

Actualization based on a four-million-franc investment

I propose that we base our projections for the actualization of a European-American settlement project in Texas on a capital investment of four-million-francs, disbursed progressively.

The Settlement Agency is responsible for gathering the headrights for an area measuring roughly four hundred square leagues or sixteen hundred hectares; the current value represents four hundred thousand francs. At the same time, the Settlement Agency also sends a committee, that must include a geologist, to explore the northern and western regions of Texas. The land must include areas in proximity to waterways that allow access to the coast in order to facilitate and establish transportation and communication networks.

In addition, we will also establish an account containing two hundred forty thousand francs to fund future land acquisition. Based on the rate of forty-two hundred francs per square league per dozen settlers, we would add two hundred square leagues to our initial settlement to accommodate twenty-four hundred incoming immigrants.

Note: Given the scale of our project, it is highly probable that the State of Texas will grant parcels of lands to the Settlement Agency. In this case, a portion of the monies that were earmarked for the purchase of lands can be directed toward other expenditures.

While these preliminary measures are underway, I will begin the administrative tasks related to your inquiries prompted by the publication of my Report, all of which must be catalogued and responded to, so we can approximate the number of initial settlers and schedule successive departures as well as the procurement and shipment of needed goods. Once we obtain these preliminary numbers, we can better estimate and plan for the scale of preparations needed for the settlement site.

We will determine the characteristics of the architectural units based on local environmental and climactic considerations. I propose that we base these units on what the architect Jean-Nicolas-Louis Durand calls *entre-axes*, which will greatly simplify construction as this method relies on the patterned repetition of specific architectural elements. One can look to the Crystal Palace in London to better understand the expression of this type of architecture. If we follow this methodology, we will ensure that our buildings can be adapted to the practical needs of our community while remaining scalable as well as varied, yet homogenous and symmetrical.

The Americans, responsible for guiding the cohort of pioneers entrusted to prepare the land prior to the arrival of the first group of settlers, will receive the drafts and execute the plans. It is understood that this first operation will include the preparation of a community center as well as the fabrication of various outposts that will serve to establish our main lines of communication and transport. It might well benefit us to situate our main settlement along a navigable river, or at the very l   east, as close as possible to one.

According to this line of thought, the preparation phase should not last more than one year from the time the first cohort of pioneers arrives in Texas. I estimate that the following year we should be able to accommodate the arrival of twelve hundred settlers, including men, women, and children.

Let us estimate that we will contract one hundred fifty workers, for one year, in order to complete the preparations; this would seem to be a sufficient number. These workers will include Germans from Ohio and New Orleans, Americans from the Western and Northern United States, as well as a certain number of workers from Europe, who will go through a proper vetting process. The Americans we hire to manage the preparatory phase will be in charge of hiring the workers, except for those who will join them directly from Europe.

Let us reason that we will incur the following costs:

wages, food, and transport of 150 men	300,000 francs
mills and mechanical saws	50,000
tools for carpentry, masonry and smithery	20,000
tools for agriculture, harnesses, carts, harrows, spades, etc . . .	10,000
carriages, chariots and various other fixtures used for transport	23,000

construction supplies, seeds, nursery, and garden supplies	170,000

These numbers might be a little exaggerated, however, the categories of products are all indispensable.

Although it is not crucial, we might consider the immediate purchase of animals to populate the surrounding prairie. Let us therefore stipulate the cost of our herds:

2,000 heads of cattle (1600 cows and 400 steer)	100,000 francs
1,000 colts and mares (sourced from Mexico)	80,000
farm animals (mules, sheep, hogs, fowl, etc . . .)	60,000

We should lend serious consideration to the fabrication of tanks, vats, barrels, clay pipes, as well as the construction of a tannery, a brewery, and a creamery. For this purpose, let us estimate the following expenditures: 75,000 francs.

The first-year costs that pertain to the above-mentioned expenditures amount to 1,540,000 francs.

If you subtract the 240,000 francs to fund future land acquisition, we are left with 1,300,000 francs.

If the State of Texas grants us acreage, we will save 900 000 francs.

Nevertheless, let us count on the sum of 1,300,000 francs for the total expenditures during our first year.

For the second year, let us estimate the following costs:

transportation to Texas for American and
European settlers   100 000 francs
furnishings for all domestic and
commercial establishments   600 000

The total amount for our expenditures for the first and second year amounts to 2 000 000 francs.

What remains is a total of 2 000 000 francs that will be used toward the following expenses:

establishment of new businesses; purchase of new machinery; acquisition of livestock and acreage; continued support for new settlers.

This estimate should amply meet our current needs; a more detailed account would not provide any additional value for the preparation of our mission, and any attempt to compile an elaboration of detailed costs would simply be a waste of our time. Therefore, if we venture to accept this general framework, we accept that, beginning in the second year, we will be fully ready to welcome the first waves of immigrants. Upon arriving, they will encounter extensive areas of productive farmland, stocked warehouses, flourishing gardens, livestock and farm animals. Aside from the orchards that will not have had time to mature, the agricultural and horticultural structures will be fully operative.

XXV

The first structures in Texas will be fashioned in the manner of the shacks built by American pioneers: horizontally stacked tree trunks for the walls and overlaid boards supported by beams for the roof. Since wood is abundant and the men will have access to mechanical saws, this process is both economical and quite expeditious. These buildings, hugged by the vast Texas sky, will provide very comfortable abodes and, with some attention to details, they can be arranged into an aesthetically pleasing assemblage. In addition to lumber, we can easily access native limestone whose use is both decorative and practical since it hardens like plaster.

The ground floor of each pavilion includes a veranda or a covered area to provide shade. These covered passages connect the various buildings; they can be enhanced with gravel walkways lined with decorative flower beds and bushes. Decorative, fragrant vines will wrap around the posts that support the roofs of the porticos; mature lianas will carpet the walls of buildings just as ivies embellish the exteriors of our homes in Europe.

This hovering vegetation combined with the lightness of the structures will create a harmonious space that radiates charm and architectural finesse. Indeed, the natural beauty of North Texas, with its woods, rivers, streams, and boundless prairies, will further accentuate the allure of our communities, especially if we pay attention to precisely marry our structures with apt picturesque locations.

Since our domestic animals will live on the open prairie, and the fields do not need to be fertilized, there will be little need to erect assorted agricultural buildings. The maintenance of public spaces requires minimal resources.

Our original herd will quickly expand, and will provide an ample source of nutrition. Few animals will be used in the fields since we will most likely use machines to assist us in agriculture production. What's more, we will have access to an abundance of game.

The advance contingents will have established a communications system and outlined a trade network based on direct relationships between producers and consumers in Europe and America. Our settlement will own its own steamship service, either by contracting with an existing company or by acquisition of its own boats.

You can deduce from the details in the preceding paragraphs that our plan is not to have the settlers face hardships upon their arrival. They will not be left to their own devices to battle nature and face the unknown. Instead, they will encounter comfortable homes, sufficient provisions, and all the necessary accoutrements to begin their work, all while enjoying the magnificent Texas climate. In short, they will have all the necessary elements to immediately become active participants in this new social experiment.

The future is ensured: nobody will be burdened by the relentless need to right the inequities imposed by society.

Instead of a life consumed by cruel insecurities, we will finally conquer the right to claim the integral role that each one of us, individually, occupies in society; this is what Fourier referred to as insouciance. It represents our right to exist in a social capacity, the right to live in harmony with the people and the elements that surround us. Each member of our society will become part of a social body founded by common principals that will integrate each aspect of our daily existence.

The inevitability of success; the rapid development of our collective prosperity; the growth resulting from the fruits of our labor; the responsiveness of the surrounding natural elements: all these factors contribute to our faith in our future and constitute the *dawn of joy*. I am well aware of the authority of this communication, and I chose to use it without restraint.

The presence of fundamental happiness is tangible in these propitious regions! On several occasions, when we visited outposts along the frontier, we met women who were brought up in the cultured and elegant milieus of Eastern capitals. Each of these women maintained that there was no place they would rather live, even though their lives lacked certain luxuries and their social circles were minimal. One of these women, the wife of a Commander posted for two years in Fort Worth, declared that her only desire was to spend another ten years in the area.

When we discussed our project, nobody doubted its success nor the exhilaration the settlers would experience.

Truthfully, if one puts aside the more difficult and arduous tasks, such as laboring in the fields, it is easy to recognize the positive outcomes of life in a society seeped in freedom, where the richness of social interaction is encouraged and the elegance of a collective society is valued, and all seek to live in harmony within their social sphere.

If we follow this elaborated plan, the preliminary phase will be brief. After the preparations are complete, during the first six months we would see to the settlement of the population charged with agricultural development and other necessary trades. During the following six months, we would begin to welcome all those involved with education, artisans, and other activities related to the social enhancement of our settlement. With this, we will enter our second phase.

While we undertake these exploits, we must likewise tend to our future *affaires*. We can assume that our community will continue to grow and that we will acquire a printing press that allows us to publish a paper in which we share new developments and also expound our ideas. A significant portion of our future *affaires* centers around the logistics that will facilitate the sustained arrival of settlers. We must ensure the establishment and the oversight of a secure and easy passage on water and on land. This will involve the creation of regularly distanced stations, such as country stores, where travelers can rest and acquire supplies.

XXVI

Up to this point, we tried to predict the various cooperative agreements that settlers might want to proposition in order to preserve each person's total freedom of choice. At this time, I propose to define the types of agreements that we might encounter.

It is typical to begin an endeavor, such as the one we plan to undertake in Texas, by disseminating a small number of settlers across a vast expanse of land. We shan't dwell on the reasons behind this conventional arrangement; suffice it to say that this mode is regrettable from the standpoint of sociability since continued isolation tends to produce an inferior social structure and will eventually lead to complete lack of social association.

In the case of our settlement mission, the underlying sentiments and ideology of our followers provide us meaningful assurance that this type of dispersion will not occur. Nevertheless, some persons, who become inspired to join our mission to Texas upon reading this report, might be disposed to settle autonomously, either within the area of our purview, or outside this area entirely. This does not matter as these settlers will act exclusively for themselves, and wherever they decide to remain, they will not detract from our ability to bring forth our mission. If they chose to live on lands not owned by us, they contribute to the population effort and also to the expansion of trade. If they chose to settle on our land so as to benefit from the proximity to our centers of operations, they will contribute even more directly to our commercial activities thus increasing the worth of our territory.

You might wonder if some will object to these private settlements; if we welcome them so effortlessly, will this detract from our own use of the land intended for our collective enterprises? According to our plan, we will purchase more land than we initially require; we will begin with the settlement of areas that can accommodate substantial initiatives capable of annexing one square league for each twelve men that arrive and intend to participate in our collective community.

Let us not forget that we can also profit from the sale of land parcels as their value increases. This income can contribute significantly to the growth of our capital, and we can then invest these resources back into our collective enterprises. Hence, we must not impede or fear the development of these remote, individual settlements; rather, our communities should welcome them and indeed we should support them with generous concessions.

Let me stress that we will not be deprived of land. As our settlements expand, we will acquire more virgin land, and we will also yield certain areas, if we deem this profitable. The quest for new land will become second nature and could indeed develop into a shared and lucrative activity.

To conclude our considerations in regard to these isolated settlements, let us consider the fundamental nature of our mission: the successful creation of an Associative Society. With this in mind, we must have faith that the individuals who dwell in remote settlements might gravitate, of their own free will, toward our collective communities, as they come to recognize all the advantages that our society has to offer.

As to the settlers who are inspired to follow our mission but prefer to remain somewhat isolated, they will be disposed to establish a system of contractual agreements with our collective community, thus achieving a greatly evolved and practical form of socialism. Even if this were to become the predominant model, it would constitute a system based on reciprocal and collective guarantees.

I have consistently advocated a system in which active and absolute freedom predominates because this freedom is the elemental principle of our theory. We pursue the model of *Association*, but, in the text of our doctrine, there is no need to preface this with the word *voluntary*, since Association represents convergence based on free will. Yet it is not sufficient to proclaim that individuals deliberately choose to associate of their own free will at a given moment in time; they must remain free to make this a persistent and deliberate choice. This implies that individuals retain the theoretical and pragmatic right to distance themselves from the Association at any point in time.

XXVII

1/ The assurance of active freedom is intrinsically desirable

As discussed above, the role it plays within the scope of our mission is evident; it applies to every aspect of our undertaking. For those participants who are not drawn to our cause's social objectives, active freedom becomes indispensable: without it, their participation would be difficult to imagine. For those participants whose goals align with our mission, more specifically with our phalansterian objectives, active freedom retains a great deal of value as it ensures their ability to make choices based on their individual preferences and guarantees full jurisdiction over individual prosperity and future prospects.

Indeed, this freedom formally draws socialist disciples to our cause. While their practices and theories differ from ours, we invite them to join us in our wide-open field that welcomes all progressive doctrines. They would not heed our call if not for the assurance that they are free to design and develop their own strategies as they see fit. In our grand haven, open to all forms of progressive ideas of our century, each doctrine bestows rewards as each contributes in varied ways to the objectives of our new society. Even the most flawed ideas benefit the prodigious cause of Truth and Humanity. Together, these progressive ideas provide varied insights into daily life, work and collective prosperity, and they shape our collective experience. Through trial and error, we will learn which concepts to apply in order to create visible and tangible realities that will substantiate and nurture Truth.

The assurance of active freedom sustains another, no less important, characteristic.

XXVIII

2/ The assurance of active freedom can facilitate the success of collective societies founded on a sound theoretical basis.

This statement might appear to contradict my previous
comments in which I argue against the belief that the success of our settlement must rest on the establishment of a
phalanstery. I remain opposed to the preconceived idea that
the phalanstery is the only means by which we can begin
our collective society; we should not constrain ourselves by
imposing such a condition.

We must consider our experiences before we make decisions. Let us observe our daily environment and empiri-
cally determine our needs. Instead of enclosing our social
experiment in a boiler devoid of a pressure valve, let us unre-
strict our experiment and allow it to interact freely with its
surroundings.

Now that I have outlined the essential differences in the
principles of these two applications, I will elaborate on the
reasons why I support the latter.

Earlier in the report, we mentioned how settlers might
initially decide to take advantage of the ease of replicat-
ing analogous collective settlements, such as the N.A. Ph.
We can therefore envision how this establishment can be
expanded to our land in Texas, where its members could

consort with a vigorous, eager population. They will also encounter conditions that are entirely favorable to their community's growth. Indeed, the climate alone presents a great advantage since, during the long winter months, the members of the N.A. Ph. subsist in a wholly lethargic state.

We will likely witness the rapid growth of our community, given the propitious conditions in Texas, especially in the area of agriculture. This will inevitably lead to the growth of personal as well as collective prosperity, which will serve as powerful and effectual motivation since all the settlers will ascertain the realization of our objective. Undeniably, if one spends any length of time at the N.A. Ph., one notices the prevailing defeatist attitude among its members; there exists little hope among them that they are capable of meeting their objective.

The N.A. Ph. succumbed to the exact impasse that I previously discussed. Their present weakness consists of their insistence to constitute their mission on a preconceived notion without estimating the conditions or considering the impediments that might arise from their surroundings. If we transpose the N.A. Ph. to our site in Texas, its members will immediately recognize that they joined forces with a critical mission, and this in turn will awaken a newfound purpose. If this were to be the case, this group could conceivably become the embryonic element of our mission, and the energy produced by its activity will nourish and nurture the growth of our society.

It is certain that a large number of our first settlers will likely elect to immediately institute a plan for a collective society comparable to the N.A. Ph.; however, our plan for a collective Order will rest on a much broader base and its nature will be eminently more flexible. Individuals who joined the N.A. Ph were expected to become full-fledged members of the movement within a certain timeframe, otherwise they are required to leave; there exists no intermediary status. This lack of flexibility caused a group to splinter from the N.A. Ph in order to found a settlement at Raritan Bay. We propose to allow individuals the choice to join our settlement fully or partially, and we will even encourage residents to form independent workshops or businesses. Based on our observations, these are the preferred conditions to offer our settlers.

The structure we outlined here does not correspond to the collective community experience; rather, it corresponds to a broader definition of a settlement, hence the settlers will not begin their new lives with an amplified sense of hope that is susceptible to causing unwelcome despondency if they become discouraged. On the other hand, the development of individual enterprises will not interfere with the development of a collective community since the individuals who seek a communal structure will remain engaged and those who prefer more independence will not be eschewed. With this arrangement, nobody will feel excluded since individuals will be free to pursue various degrees of social involvement. As happens with natural organisms, our integral elements will innately gravitate toward the actions that correspond to their natural inclinations.

XXIX

I have already written about the difference in temperament between Anglo-Americans and those of us with Latin roots. Americans and the French in particular are quite complementary; I expect certain distinctive French traits will be tempered by the intermingling of the two races. The French penchant for boastfulness and for superficial vanity, their tendency to criticize indiscriminately and brazenly, and their susceptibility to engage in foolish arguments will, to a certain degree, acquiesce when confronted with the calm, levelheaded demeanor of enterprising Americans. One hopes this will result in the redirection of this energy toward more suitable and productive matters.

Americans will also benefit from certain modifications to their characteristic dispositions. The French will enlighten Americans in matters of social skills, art, refinement, and in matters that pertain to human emotion in general. In this important mission of communal education, the French settlers should be mindful of not exposing strong individual discrepancies so as to avoid being discredited and consequently ignored by the very people to whom they hope to impart a high degree of sociability.

American women are fully conscious of their personal rights and of their autonomy, in contrast to French women who in reality remain subjugated. The pursuit of personal freedom is a universal, lifelong pastime in America. In fact, a young American woman of fifteen has far more freedom to act than an eighteen-year-old French man who comes from a good family: she can go out and about alone, and when it pleases her; she maintains her own social circles and enjoys outings with her friends. She is treated respectfully when she travels independently and does not have to fear indiscreet chatter. She remains fully aware of her autonomy and of her freedom.

Nonetheless, young American women are admonished for their lack of charm and their emotive immaturity. In our old-world view, these shortcomings are the result of the spirit I described above. Instead, the real cause rests in the ultra-puritanical origins of the United States, the overall lack of sufficiently sophisticated social skills, and finally in American men's universal preoccupation with business and *making money*. If American women impart autonomy and self-awareness to young European women, in exchange, they can expect to cultivate their scarce sensitivity and the social skills they require. The results of these exchanges will benefit all those involved.

This complementary reciprocity so evident in matters of collective sociability can be equally applied to both speculative and theoretical ideological matters. On these issues, the disposition of Europeans is swayed by accounts of a civilization seeped in history and philosophy, whereas the Anglo-Americans reveal a more innovative and ingenious spirit. This approach will quickly dismiss the vagaries of European metaphysics and demonstrate to the Europeans that, in practice, all ideas conceived by man are in fact pragmatically achievable.

In short, I have always rejected the idea of an associative experiment in Europe where families are brought together to live in close quarters, under restrictive and inflexible conditions. For this reason, I conclude by emphasizing that we should not prematurely enact the objectives of any social theory; rather, we should initially focus on our settlement in and of itself in order to ensure its stable growth, and the realization of our collective society will follow. In fact, the progress of our society will be facilitated by the very fact that we will allow individuals to develop various associative models, and to maintain the freedom to dissolve these connections at any time.

Collective enterprises are undoubtedly better equipped to serve the needs of newly arrived settlers who would turn to them for supplies and all their other immediate needs. Even if in their minds they intend to rely on these centers only temporarily, social and commercial exchanges will occur spontaneously. Within ten years, everyone will realize that a collective society is perfectly compatible with an individual's freedom in personal and family matters. Indeed, as the settlers who arrived with the intention of establishing an autonomous settlement become more rooted in the collective enterprise and benefit from its countless advantages, I would not be surprised if many of them chose to remain within the collective society.

At this juncture, I imagine that you no longer harbor

any doubts in regard to the importance of founding well-organized and robust early settlements that follow the directives outlined in the previous sections of the report. The success of these early settlements will provide a solid foundation for and enable the promotion of the collective society. Further, this will ensure the development of prosperity that will in turn lead to the advancement of the concepts that will uphold the structure of this new collective.

XXX

Once the agricultural and trade enterprises have taken root, the second phase begins and it is time to welcome the settlers apt to fulfill the functions related to all matters of social enhancement. As we previously discussed, this phase would take place during the second half of the first year of settlement. The configuration of the community's cultural and civic life will include the creation of artistic and scientific institutions, as well as other elements that will encourage all types of social interactions.

Once our first community is established and can receive additional settlers, we will dispatch groups of workers to plan new communities. These will be elaborated without much difficulty since we will program the creation of these centers progressively, in accordance with the number of new arrivals. As the cooperative centers multiply, so will the commercial and social connections among the groups of settlers. This expansion will promote the improvement of procedures and enterprises which will eventually bring forth a perfected model of a harmonized collective society.

Over the period of roughly three years, we will establish our first community and the regular development of other cooperative groups will evolve. At this time, in these ideal conditions, social experimentation will begin to take place. You might all wonder if this sequence of events would not be possible in Europe, if we could chance a similar mission on more familiar territory. I have made my decision: in a few months, I will be on the road to Texas. The realization of the mission to which I have dedicated my life will take place in no other place on earth. I am going. In fact, I no longer ask myself if this will happen; currently I am simply concerned with the scale of the project, and this my friends, depends on you and your support.

XXXI

I would be remiss if I did not enlighten you about the subsequent and manifest consequences of the society that we will found.

When we don't travel extensively, we tend to suffer from European myopia. What do I mean by this? Well, since Europe has existed for so many centuries, we see it as the center of the universe, and that it is the only place where one can play the great game of Human Destiny. We are sclerotic in our ability to recognize that the world progresses outside of our borders, and we are loath to accept any changes that occur "too far away," meaning too far from us. In our time, this is nothing more than a parochial prejudice. It would take merely two hours spent in New York, Boston, or Philadelphia to change the mind of even the most devoted Europeanist. Below are my thoughts for those of you who did not have the opportunity to experience those two hours.

At this moment, we will no longer question the actual success of our mission. We will consider the objections from a different perspective. Let us assume that we succeed: we found our new society; the process of seriisme is put into place and functions according to the propositions advanced in its theoretical design. To what extent will these developments influence the world? We can expect this question: "Isn't the proving ground too far removed from civilization and the great sphere where all the most important issues that concern the future of civilization are resolved?" Can we assert that we proved our success if we choose to conduct this experiment in this far-flung land? How will this benefit humanity?

Let us review: we have succeeded, we have founded a new society. What does this signify? Let us now examine this theoretical train of thought and the conclusions we can draw.

The population in our settlements has reached a significant mass, and the numbers continue to increase. These settlers brought with them their expertise in a variety of industries, and they also applied the most innovative scientific methods to their work. Further, they contributed their progressive ideas to the economic and social development of our society.

Thanks to our labor, the virgin farmland that we acquired has become extremely productive and valuable. We are utilizing the gains from the land to develop more settlement sites that are becoming profitable in and of themselves.

We have established effective and rapid communication pathways with the main American commercial hubs.

Our landholdings have increased tenfold thanks to our implementation of a two-step process. First, we profited from the sale of the land adjacent to the first settlements, next, we continued to expand into remote areas; the development of these lands in fact became one of our settlements' thriving enterprises.

Meanwhile, the population of the surrounding areas continues to increase significantly, thanks in part to the arrival of railroad and telegraph lines. The arts, the sciences, leisure activities and all other elements of a refined society have flourished in our settlements; the vibrancy of a new civilization pulsates through the air. This tangible progress is the result of the experimentation we conducted with the expectation that we would find solutions to social problems developed over centuries. This New Order embodies the practical expressions of our theories and our ideas. Our society creates and acts; it grows; it communicates and trades with the outside world; it lives and shines.

And, pray tell, where is this wonderous center located? It is situated in a central region of the United States of America, the only country in the world where a young, vigorous, enlightened and truly modern population thrives in its surroundings. To the contrary, since the beginning of the century, European civilizations have continued to veer from peaceful and congruent issues. Admittedly, it would be useful to outline the current state of affairs in Europe; however, I cannot opine on this substantial question at the moment. Suffice it to say that we should individually reflect on the subject.

Myriad unrelenting antagonisms continue to erode European society. The description that Fourier penned in the epilogue of his 1808 work, *The Theory of the Four Movements,* holds truer today than at his writing. We have witnessed the prelude to the social wars that have percolated over the past eighteen years. What could bring about the resolution, or better yet the dissolution, of these severe hostilities? This is a somber question indeed.

While Europe is thus engaged, America endeavors to prepare its role, which in my view, is no longer hypothetical. Today, America has become the beacon of the Occident, and she will usher our world into a new era. This same process occurred centuries ago, albeit at a much slower pace: what Europe was to Asia, America is now to Europe. Indeed, if one observes the progression of civilization, it evolved not just through time, but also through space. The impulses for evolution always advanced from the Orient to the Occident, just like the sun. American society has its roots in our Greco-Roman civilization, which in turn was rooted in Egypt and Asia. This circular nature of this journey suggests that the next evolutionary point for humanity will alight in America where it will end its voyage. We can certainly perceive ample evidence of this principle.

Europe's persistent preoccupation with war is one of the elements that contributes to America's ascendancy over our society. For decades, Europe dedicated itself almost exclusively to the planning of conquests. Certainly, there has been progress in science, industry, and commerce; however, the elaboration of these innovations was hindered by Europe's ancient conflicts and its pervasive tradition of violence. On the contrary, the American society was founded on those modern elements that Europe eschewed; consequently, as Europe continues to be mired in discords and battles, Europeans can turn to the pristine, unrestricted land that beckons them to fulfill their aspirations.

I invite you to turn your attention to the following charts

I copied from a book about the United States written by M. Goodrich, the ex-consul of the United States in Paris. You will find they provide peremptory evidence to support my thesis about America.

POPULATION GROWTH IN PRINCIPAL US CITIES

PRINCIPALES VILLES.	1790	1800	1810	1820	1830	1840	1850
Portland (Maine)	»	3 677	7 169	8 581	12 601	15 218	26 819
Bangor	»	»	850	1 221	2 867	8 627	14 441
Manchester (New-Ham.)	»	»	615	761	877	3 235	18 933
Boston (Massach.)	18 038	24 027	32 250	43 298	61 392	93 383	138 788
Lowel	»	»	»	»	6 474	20 796	32 964
Springfield	»	»	2 767	3 914	6 784	10 085	21 602
Salem	7 921	9 457	12 613	12 721	13 886	15 082	18 846
Lawrence	»	»	»	»	»	»	18 341
Providence (Rh. Isl.)	»	7 614	10 071	11 767	16 832	23 171	41 513
New-Haven (Connect.)	»	»	5 772	7 147	10 180	14 890	22 539
Hartford	»	»	3 955	4 726	7 074	12 793	17 966
New-York (N. Y.)	33 131	60 489	96 373	123 706	203 007	312 710	515 394
Brooklyn	»	3 298	4 402	7 175	12 042	36 223	96 850
Albany	3 498	5 349	9 356	12 630	24 238	33 721	50 771
Buffalo	»	»	1 508	2 095	8 653	18 213	40 266
Rochester	»	»	»	1 502	9 269	20 191	36 561
Williamsburg	»	»	»	»	1 620	5 680	30 786
Troy	»	»	3 885	5 264	11 401	19 334	28 785
Syracuse	»	»	»	»	»	6 502	22 235
Utica	»	»	»	2 972	8 323	12 783	17 240
Newark (New-Jers.)	»	»	»	6 507	10 953	17 296	38 885
Paterson	»	»	»	»	»	7 596	21 341
Philadelphia (Pensyl.)	42 520	70 287	96 664	108 116	167 188	258 037	409 353
Pittsburg	»	1 565	4 768	7 248	12 542	21 115	50 519
Baltimore (Maryl.)	13 503	26 614	46 555	62 738	80 625	134 379	169 012
Washington	»	3 210	8 205	13 247	18 827	23 364	40 001
Richmond (Virg.)	»	5 537	9 738	12 046	16 060	20 153	27 483
Charleston (Car. du S.)	16 359	18 712	24 711	24 480	30 289	29 261	42 806
Savannah (Georgie)	»	»	»	7 523	9 748	11 214	27 841
Mobile (Alab.)	»	»	»	»	3 194	12 672	20 513
Nashville (Tenn.)	»	»	»	»	5 566	6 929	17 502
Louisville (Kent.)	»	»	1 357	4 012	10 352	21 210	43 217
Cincinnati (Ohio)	»	750	2 540	9 644	24 831	46 448	116 108
Columbus	»	»	»	»	2 435	6 048	17 367
Cleveland	»	»	547	606	1 076	6 071	17 074
Détroit (Mich.)	»	»	»	1 422	2 222	9 102	21 057
Chicago	»	»	»	»	»	4 479	28 269
Milwaukie (Wisc.)	»	»	»	»	»	1 700	20 026
Saint-Louis (Miss.)	»	»	»	4 598	5 852	16 469	82 744
Nouv.-Orléans (Louisiane)	»	»	17 242	27 176	46 310	102 193	119 285
San Francisco (Calif.)	»	»	»	»	»	»	25 000

PROGRESS IN US SPANNING 50 YEARS[1]

ANNÉES.		1793	1851
Nombre des Etats.		15	31
Recettes du Trésor. . . . . dollars		5 720 624	43 774 848
Dépenses de l'Etat. . . . . dol.		7 529 575	39 355 268
Importations. . . . . dol.		31 000 000	178 138 318
Exportation . . . . dol.		26 109 000	151 898 720
Tonnage de la marine marchande.		520 764	3 535 454
Etendue des Etats-Unis en mille carrés.		805 461	3 314 365
Personnel de l'armée.		5 120	10 000
Milice enrôlée		»	2 006 456
Marine des Etats-Unis (vaisseaux).		(aucun)	76
— armement (artillerie).		»	2 012
Phares et bateaux-phares.		12	372
Milles de chemins de fer en activité		»	10 287
Dépense desdits		»	306 607 954
Milles de chemins de fer en construction		»	10 092
Lignes télégraphiques, en milles		»	15 000
Nombre des bureaux de poste		209	21 551
Milles de routes de poste		5 642	178 762
Revenu des postes . . . . dollars		104 747	5 592 971
Dépense du département des postes . . . doll.		72 040	5 212 953
Nombre de milles des transports		»	46 541 425
Collèges.		19	121
Bibliothèques publiques		35	695
Volumes de la bibliothèque		75 000	2 201 632
Bibliothèque des écoles.		»	10 000
Volumes de ces bibliothèques		»	2 000 000
Emigrants de l'Europe aux Etats-Unis		10 000	315 333
Fabrication des minerais . . . . dollars		9 664	52 019 465

These charts provide extremely useful historical summaries. The figures demonstrate that growth in all areas, from population to the sale of public lands, seems destined to continue at a remarkably swift pace. The sale of public land

---

1. The above information is taken from a speech delivered on July 4, 1852, in Washington, by Mr. Webster, Secretary of State.

quintupled in one year! This sharp increase is due to the expansion of the railroad, the most notable development known to man to date. The new world's capacity to absorb immigrants from Europe is astonishing; this movement of people who flee the political and social troubles in Europe is facilitated by the sustained improvement of travel.

To better recognize the draw of the United States, let us consider the following analogy; humans, especially those from civilized countries, exist as a liquid mass whose movements along the surface of earth are impelled by two opposite forces, a force that attracts and a force that repels. America acts as a giant mechanism that generates an accelerated force of attraction, whereas Europe's force repels.

The United States attract for many reasons: seemingly limitless land; social and political freedom; economic momentum, and innovative industry. On the other hand, Europe repels because of its general state of poverty; the high cost of land; job instability and low wages; disproportionate spending on the military; the constant and imminent threat of war; and the chronic state of instability. Our society is currently polarized, and we can summarize this current state in the following manner: on the one hand we have Old Europe, and on the other we have the New World.

People are flocking to the new states of California and Oregon; soon the area known as Utah will become a state; the railroad that connects the Atlantic and Pacific coasts will presently be joined together. The population of the continental United States is estimated to grow from fifty million people twenty-five years from now to one hundred million by the end of the century. The immense valleys of the Mississippi and Missouri rivers, formerly the western boundaries of the United States, will welcome many of these newcomers.

This brief overview should suffice to convince you that we must straightway decide to become part of this historic human enterprise that is unfolding in the United States of America.

XXXII

These final few words are not of my own writing.

[...] After the birth of a human being his early years are obscurely spent in the toils or pleasures of childhood. As he grows up the world receives him, when his manhood begins, and he enters into contact with his fellows. He is then studied for the first time, and it is imagined that the germ of the vices and the virtues of his maturer years is then formed. This, if I am not mistaken, is a great error. We must begin higher up; we must watch the infant in its mother's arms; we must see the first images which the external world casts upon the dark mirror of his mind; the first occurrences which he witnesses; we must hear the first words which awaken the sleeping powers of thought, and stand by his earliest efforts, if we would understand the prejudices, the habits, and the passions which will rule his life. The entire man is, so to speak, to be seen in the cradle of the child.

The growth of nations presents something analogous to this: they all bear some marks of their origin; and the circumstances which accompanied their birth and contributed to their rise affect the whole term of their being. If we were able to go back to the elements of states, and to examine the oldest monuments of their history, I doubt not that we should discover the primal cause of the prejudices, the habits, the ruling passions, and, in short, of all that constitutes what is called the national character; we should then find the explanation of certain customs which now seem at variance with the prevailing manners; of such laws as conflict with established principles; and of such incoherent opinions as are here and there to be met with in society, like those fragments of broken chains which we sometimes see hanging from the vault of an edifice, and supporting nothing. This might explain the destinies of certain nations, which seem borne on by an unknown force to ends of which they themselves are ignorant. But hitherto facts have been wanting to researches of this kind: the spirit of inquiry has only come upon communities in their latter days; and when they at length contemplated their origin, time had already obscured it, or ignorance and pride adorned it with truth-concealing fables.

America is the only country in which it has been possible to witness the natural and tranquil growth of society, and where the influences exercised on the future condition of states by their origin is clearly distinguishable. [...] [3]

[...] Virginia received the first English colony; the emigrants took possession of it in 1607. The idea that mines of gold and silver are the sources of national wealth was at that time singularly prevalent in Europe; a fatal delusion, which has done more to impoverish the nations which adopted it, and has cost more lives in America than the united influence of war and bad laws. The men sent to Virginia were seekers of gold, adventurers, without resources and without character, whose turbulent and restless spirit endangered the infant colony, and rendered its progress uncertain. The artisans and agriculturists arrived afterwards; and, although they were a more moral and orderly race of men, they were in nowise above the level of the inferior classes in England. No lofty conceptions, no intellectual system, directed the foundation of these new settlements. The colony was scarcely established when slavery was introduced, and this was the main circumstance which has exercised so prodigious an influence on the character, the laws, and all the future prospects of the South. Slavery, as we shall afterwards show, dishonors labor; it introduces idleness into society, and with idleness, ignorance and pride, luxury, and distress. It enervates the powers of the mind, and benumbs the activity of man. The influence of slavery, united to the English character, explains the manners and the social condition of the Southern States.

In the North, the same English foundation was modified by the most opposite shades of character; and here I may be allowed to enter into some details. The two or three main ideas which constitute the basis of the social theory of the United States were first combined in the northern English colonies, more generally denominated the States of New England. The principles of New England spread at first to the neighboring states; they then passed successively to the more distant ones; and at length they imbued the whole Confederation. They now extend their influence beyond its limits over the whole American world. The civilization of New England has been like a beacon lit upon a hill, which, after it has diffused its warmth around, tinges the distant horizon with its glow.

The foundation of New England was a novel spectacle, and all the circumstances attending it were singular and original. The large majority of colonies have been first inhabited either by men without education and without resources, driven by their poverty and their misconduct from the land which gave them birth, or by speculators and adventurers greedy of gain. [. . .]

[. . .] The settlers who established themselves on the shores of New England all belonged to the more independent classes of their native country. Their union on the soil of America at once presented the singular phenomenon of a society containing neither lords nor common people, neither rich nor poor. These men possessed, in proportion to their number, a greater mass of intelligence than is to be found in any European nation of our own time. All, without a single exception, had received a good education, and many of them were known in Europe for their talents and their acquirements. The other colonies had been founded by adventurers without family; the emigrants of New England brought with them the best elements of order and morality—they landed in the desert accompanied by their wives and children. But what most especially distinguished them was the aim of their undertaking. They had not been obliged by necessity to leave their country; the social position they abandoned was one to be regretted, and their means of subsistence were certain. Nor did they cross the Atlantic to improve their situation or to increase their wealth; the call which summoned them from the comforts of their homes was purely intellectual; and in facing the inevitable sufferings of exile their object was the triumph of an idea. The emigrants, or, as they deservedly styled themselves, the Pilgrims, belonged to that English sect the austerity of whose principles had acquired for them the name of Puritans. Puritanism was not merely a religious doctrine, but it corresponded in many points with the most absolute democratic and republican theories. It was this tendency which had aroused its most dangerous adversaries. Persecuted by the Government of the mother-country, and disgusted by the habits of a society opposed to the rigor of their own principles, the Puritans went forth to seek some rude and unfrequented part of the world, where they could live according to their own opinions, and worship God in freedom. [...]

[...] The emigrants were about one hundred fifty in number, including the women and the children. Their object was to plant a colony on the shores of the Hudson; but after having been driven about for some time in the Atlantic Ocean, they were forced to land on that arid coast of New England which is now the site of the town of Plymouth. The rock is still shown on which the pilgrims disembarked. [...]

[...] It must not be imagined that the piety of the Puritans was of a merely speculative kind, or that it took no cognizance of the course of worldly affairs. Puritanism, as I have already remarked, was scarcely less a political than a religious doctrine. No sooner had the emigrants landed on the barren coast described by Nathaniel Morton than it was their first care to constitute a society, by passing the following Act:

> "In the name of God. Amen. We, whose names are underwritten, the loyal subjects of our dread Sovereign Lord King James, etc., etc., Having undertaken for the glory of God, and advancement of the Christian Faith, and the honour of our King and country, a voyage to plant the first colony in the northern parts of Virginia; Do by these presents solemnly and mutually, in the presence of God and one another, covenant and combine ourselves together into a civil body politick, for our better ordering and preservation, and furtherance of the ends aforesaid: and by virtue hereof do enact, constitute and frame such just and equal laws, ordinances, acts, constitutions, and officers, from time to time, as shall be thought most meet and convenient for the general good of the Colony: unto which we promise all due submission and obedience," etc.

This happened in 1620, and from that time forwards the emigration went on. The religious and political passions which ravaged the British Empire during the whole reign of Charles I drove fresh crowds of sectarians every year to the shores of America. In England the stronghold of Puritanism was in the middle classes, and it was from the middle classes that the majority of the emigrants came. The population of New England increased rapidly; and while the hierarchy of rank despotically classed the inhabitants of the mother-country, the colony continued to present the novel spectacle of a community homogeneous in all its parts. A democracy, more perfect than any which antiquity had dreamt of, started in full size and panoply from the midst of an ancient feudal society. [...]

[...] The chief care of the legislators, in this body of penal laws, was the maintenance of orderly conduct and good morals in the community: they constantly invaded the domain of conscience, and there was scarcely a sin which was not subject to magisterial censure. [...]

[...] These errors are no doubt discreditable to human reason; they attest the inferiority of our nature, which is incapable of laying firm hold upon what is true and just, and is often reduced to the alternative of two excesses. In strict connection with this penal legislation, which bears such striking marks of a narrow sectarian spirit, and of those religious passions which had been warmed by persecution and were still fermenting among the people, a body of political laws is to be found, which, though written two hundred years ago, is still ahead of the liberties of our age. The general principles which are the groundwork of modern constitutions—principles which were imperfectly known in Europe, and not completely triumphant even in Great Britain, in the seventeenth century—were all recognized and determined by the laws of New England: the intervention of the people in public affairs, the free voting of taxes, the responsibility of authorities, personal liberty, and trial by jury, were all positively established without discussion. From these fruitful principles consequences have been derived and applications have been made such as no nation in Europe has yet ventured to attempt. [...]

[...] If, after having cast a rapid glance over the state of American society in 1650, we turn to the condition of Europe, and more especially to that of the Continent, at the same period, we cannot fail to be struck with astonishment. On the Continent of Europe, at the beginning of the seventeenth century, absolute monarchy had everywhere triumphed over the ruins of the oligarchical and feudal liberties of the Middle Ages. Never were the notions of right more completely confounded than in the midst of the splendor and literature of Europe; never was there less political activity among the people; never were the principles of true freedom less widely circulated; and at that very time those principles, which were scorned or unknown by the nations of Europe, were proclaimed in the deserts of the New World, and were accepted as the future creed of a great people. The boldest theories of the human reason were put into practice by a community so humble that not a statesman condescended to attend to it; and a legislation without a precedent was produced offhand by the imagination of the citizens. [...]

[...] The remarks I have made will suffice to display the character of Anglo-American civilization in its true light. It is the result (and this should be constantly present to the mind of two distinct elements), which in other places have been in frequent hostility, but which in America have been admirably incorporated and combined with one another. I allude to the spirit of Religion and the spirit of Liberty. [...]

XXXIII

The map of Texas that I attached to my report shows the route of the forthcoming railroad that will enter the state at Fulton, on the Red River; it then intersects the Trinity near Athens, then continues on to Fort Gates and ends in El Paso.[11]

I mentioned that we encountered businessmen from New York who came to "see what deals can be made in Texas," and I foresee that many Northerners will soon venture to the state. The construction of the railroad will only hasten this prediction. Indeed, the Texas legislature has given generous land grants for the railroad: fifteen thousand acres for each ten thousand miles of tracks.

This rail line will cross the Mississippi River in Memphis and then run straight through the state of Arkansas. From Memphis to El Paso the distance is four hundred leagues and it will eventually stretch all the way to California. America's Southern states will undeniably become linked to the Pacific Ocean through the State of Texas. You can add this fact to what you already know about this State.

I can incontestably confirm Texas represents the best place in the world to elaborate our social experiment. Our nascent society will be among the first to occupy these barren lands, but we will soon be joined by waves of others whose analogous configurations will emerge around us. We will demonstrate the superiority of our social model in which our settlers assimilate into a harmonic Social Order, whereas to the north, we find Native Americans who were illegitimately displaced, and to the south, we find slavery, a calamitous situation that Americans seem incapable of altering.

Some might still argue that we should refrain from moving forward with our objective until we are capable of founding our new Order in Europe. Certainly, we can all agree that the most effectual and expeditious path forward consists of creating our society in an unsettled arena so as to animate our Idea and shape it into a tangible and organic reality. Even if the situation in Europe were to change from one day to the next, its social inequities would still need to be repaired, and it would be more fruitful to conduct a social experiment elsewhere before embarking on such a long and arduous process. *Qui habet aures audiendi audiat.*

It is not a matter of abandoning Europe; it is, and always will be, a way to save Europe and indeed the world.

End of the Report

NOTES

1. Consideant, Victor. *Au Texas, Deuxième Édition,* École Sociétaire, Pais, 6 de Beaume, 1855, 155–156.

2. De Tocqueville, Alexis. *Democracy in America: Volumes I and II,* Floating Press, The, 2009. *ProQuest Ebook Central,* 70–71.

3. De Tocqueville, Alexis. *Democracy in America: Volumes I and II,* Floating Press, The, 2009. *ProQuest Ebook Central,* 75–77.

4. De Tocqueville, Alexis. *Democracy in America: Volumes I and II,* Floating Press, The, 2009. *ProQuest Ebook Central,* 77–78.

5. De Tocqueville, Alexis. *Democracy in America: Volumes I and II,* Floating Press, The, 2009. *ProQuest Ebook Central,* 82.

6. De, Tocqueville, Alexis. *Democracy in America: Volumes I and II,* Floating Press, The, 2009. *ProQuest Ebook Central,* 83.

7. De, Tocqueville, Alexis. *Democracy in America: Volumes I and II,* Floating Press, The, 2009. *ProQuest Ebook Central,* 89.

8. De, Tocqueville, Alexis. *Democracy in America: Volumes I and II*, Floating Press, The, 2009. *ProQuest Ebook Central*, 91.

9. De, Tocqueville, Alexis. *Democracy in America: Volumes I and II*, Floating Press, The, 2009. *ProQuest Ebook Central*, 95.

10. De, Tocqueville, Alexis. *Democracy in America: Volumes I and II*, Floating Press, The, 2009. *ProQuest Ebook Central*, 96.

11. Consideant, Victor. *Au Texas, Deuxième Édition*, École Sociétaire, Pais, 6 de Beaume, 1855.

In America I found one of Fourier's original letters that I believe is relevant and of interest to our purpose.

To Mr. John Barnet, Consul of the United States, Paris

Paris, December 20, 1923

Dear Sir,

I believe my social theory, the creation of a Phalanx Community, would be of great interest to the United States, which is the reason why I penned this letter to you. America must control its fierce Native tribes such as the Creek and the Cherokee, etc . . . These wild tribes will not engage in agriculture unless it is presented to them as a natural and attractive order, the order of *harmonic series* that I describe in my social doctrine.

The experimental living construct that I call a phalanstery offers a more economical solution in the United States than in Europe thanks to the availability of land and the abundance of lumber. Indeed, this might be entirely appropriate for some of your smaller colonies, such as Nashville, as these buildings can accommodate up to one hundred families.

The construction of phalansteries holds another advantage for the United States: you would be in a position to welcome a steady flow of settlers from Europe. America already receives immigrants from Europe; however, their arrivals are unpredictable. If you build phalansteries, you could welcome up to three hundred thousand settlers per year from Europe and China.

The announcement of my discovery is forthcoming; however, I wanted to ensure that you receive the information contained in the enclosed summary in case the publication is postponed, as is often the case with these types of pamphlets. I have in fact personally undertaken their distribution to individual households as a means of readily diffusing the information.

Could I possibly obtain, by the agency of your goodwill, the names and the addresses of the Americans of note who currently reside in Paris, in order that I may deliver my pamphlets to their residences? I sincerely hope you do not consider my request to be a transgression, as I assumed that it would be simple task for your secretary who could convey this information to me.

I remain, most respectfully, your humble servant,

Charles Fourier
Rue Neuve-St-Roch
Hotel St-Roch

P.S. During my twenty-four years of research in the area of Associationism, I never considered describing more lower levels (p.4); I stopped at level six.

I have since determined that we can limit the initial capital expenditures to six hundred thousand Francs (Banque rurale, p.8 bis.). How accessible this will be for the United States who have such a pressing need for this innovation!

Below Fourier's original letter, I found this annotation by the Consul.

Received December 29, 1823:

> Include in my packet for the Marmion and forward to Professor Griscom without close examination. At a glance, the work appears to be either a genuine curiosity or the emanation of a disturbed brain.
>
> J.C.Barnet

The original letter is currently in the hands of M. Griscom of the N.A. Ph., the cousin of Professor Griscom, to whom M. Barnet had addressed it.

FIRST INSTRUCTIONS

FOR THOSE INDIVIDUALS WHO ARE PREPARED TO PARTICIPATE IN THE FRANCO-AMERICAN SETTLEMENT AND GO TO TEXAS

We seek individuals who are ready to help us plan and participate in our settlement mission to Texas.

This enterprise requires capital, manpower, industry, and ideas.

A.1) As the report explains, the most pressing matter is the collection of funds required to purchase land rights or land vouchers in Texas. The price of land rights continues to increase; every day it becomes more difficult and costlier to procure them. The acquisition of the vouchers will secure access to favorable parcels of land. The purchases of these vouchers can be made in the names of individual backers, even before we establish the Settlement Agency that will be responsible for the selection of the headrights in choice locations and for the organization of the settlement mission. Brisbane and several other friends are prepared to advance funds for these vouchers; these private transactions will be conducted by individuals according to their preferences. Our European friends who wish to partake in these acquisitions can transfer funds directly to the American agents who will be acting on our behalf, or they operate through European financial institutions that maintain partnerships with American counterparts. At the moment, it is imperative that those who are prepared to make these acquisitions step forward immediately so we can determine the number of registered vouchers on which we can then scale the procurement of our land rights. Small investments are welcome as the cost of land is not egregious; last summer, twenty-five francs would buy ten hectares of extremely fertile soil.

A.2) The second matter concerns the underwriting of the capital needed to constitute the Settlement Agency. The funds can be transferred in installments at a later date, once we have commissioned the agency.

B) The third matter involves the registration of those individuals who intend to participate in this operation, either from the initial planning phase, or later during the settlement process.

C) Finally, the fourth matter regards the collection and sorting of all the documentation that pertains to industries, ideas and other details germane to the settlement.

Certain forms of industry are evidently essential; however, it would be prudent to have a structure to include other optional ones as well. All industries related to agricultural production are naturally of primary standing: farming, horticulture, nurseries, viticulture and wine production, animal husbandry, dairy farming, etc . . . Industries related to construction, to production of clothing and furniture, and to metalsmithing also rank first. One need not even mention the importance all activities related to the preparation of food for consumption. We should also note that food storage and management will become increasingly prominent once we begin to establish trade agreements outside the settlement. We can expect to initiate large-scale production of salted and smoked meats, cured sausage, potted meats, etc . . .

We already mentioned the need for a tannery, a kiln, and a brewery. We should add the need for individuals skilled in following trades: metalwork, mechanics, glassblowing. It is futile to stretch out this nomenclature of technology. We can all recognize the need for specific elements, and these needs will become all the more obvious once we subsist in our new surroundings.

The Settlement Agency will execute a variety of commercial operations. We must therefore recruit not only local agents, but we must also create a network of agents in areas where they can disseminate the information contained in this report. There exists, at best, a limited presence of French and Belgian industrialists in Texas. Our settlers will be in a position to open commercial channels, hence we will require agents in Europe to develop and maintain these relationships.

D) The settlement will accept donations in kind, in addition to the underwriting of commodities. These donations can include books, art, instruments, and all sorts of products. We can attribute a value to certain goods and award them as bonuses to poor settlers who perform distinguished work, or we can gift items to children, etc . . .

Everybody involved in the settlement effort can collect kernels and seeds from plants and trees of all sorts as they will be of great use to us; everything you collect is valuable. Many varieties common in Europe are unknown in Texas where we will acclimate as many of these precious seeds as possible.

Based on the preceding information, we request that you provide us with your preliminary intents, which denotes no official engagement on your part, in regard to the following matters:

A. Capital
  (1) The financial support you are able to contribute toward the acquisition of headrights.
  (2) The financial support you are able to contribute to the establishment of the Settlement Agency; these contributions consist of consecutive installments over a period of several years.

B. Personnel
  1) Your individual readiness
  2) Information regarding other individuals who are inclined to be included among the first settlers; what skills and talents each individual can contribute, along with the person's age, profession, and health.
C. Documentation
  Those individuals who need to provide documentation to claim positions need to deliver a summary of their request immediately.
D. The donations that we intend to solicit can be categorized in advance. We hope to obtain gifts from our artist and our professional friends in particular.

A report describing the standing of the Settlement Agency has already been elaborated, and we initially intended to include it in this report; however, we decided it would be more beneficial to first collect the information that we have requested herein. This seems to be the most expeditious means to help us determine the authentic interest in our mission.

All individuals who wish to participate in this mission in any fashion must realize that they should provide us with the required information without delay. I remind you that the information you provide does not constitute a formal engagement, yet this material is essential for us to confirm the initial requirements of our mission. The British and the

Americans are fond of the expression *time is money*; how apt for our situation. We count on your speedy responses and on your eager participation.

Your replies must be addressed, postage paid, to M.C. Brunier, 2 rue de Baune, Paris.

The Paris agency is provisionally staffed by Messieurs Charles Brunier, Emile Bourdon, Allyre Bureau, Amédée Guillon. Its main function is to record all the responses received and to reply to any requests. As stated above, we will not collect any funds at the moment.

If you write from Belgium or from abroad, you can address your stamped dispatch to M.V. Considerant or to M.F. Cantagrel in Brussels.

Victor Prosper Considerant (12 October 1808–27 December 1893) was a French utopian socialist philosopher and economist. After a short service in the French army, he resigned to devote his energies to popularizing and applying the utopian ideas of Charles Fourier. Because of his participation in the abortive insurrection of June 13, 1849, against Louis Napoleon Bonaparte, Considérant was forced to flee to Brussels. There he was contacted by Albert Brisbane, an American Fourierist, who interested him in colonization efforts in Texas. Considérant visited the United States from 1852–53 and accompanied Brisbane on a trek that eventually took him through North and Central Texas. His enthusiasm for the land, climate, and people of Texas induced him to establish the European Society for the Colonization of Texas upon his return to Belgium. When La Réunion collapsed in 1859 due to financial insolvency, Considérant, discouraged but not disillusioned, moved to San Antonio, where he unsuccessfully attempted to raise funds for another commune. Unable to fulfill his dreams in Texas and still under a ban of deportation from France, he became an American citizen and farmed in Bexar County until 1869, when he and his wife returned to Paris. There he lived as a teacher and socialist sage of the Latin Quarter and died on December 27, 1893.

Paola Tettamanzi Buckley has taught foreign languages at Southern Methodist University since 2003. She is presently a Senior Lecturer in the Department of World Languages and Literature. Paola received a B.A. from Georgetown University and an M.A. from New York University. Paola worked at United Nations headquarters in New York and was accredited as both a French and Italian interpreter by the United States Department of State. She has served as an interpreter at both the White House and the Pentagon.